Moving Forward From the Past:
Early Writings and Current Reflections
of Middle School Founders

Moving Forward From the Past

Early Writings and Current Reflections of Middle School Founders

Robert David, Editor

National Middle School Association
Columbus, Ohio
&
Pennsylvania Middle School Association
Pittsburgh, Pennsylvania

NMSA

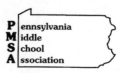

National Middle School Association	Pennsylvania Middle School Association
2600 Corporate Exchange Drive,	Box 7258
Suite 370	Pittsburgh, Pennsylvania 15213
Columbus, Ohio 43231	Telephone (412) 885-2615
Telephone (800) 528-NMSA	

NMSA

SUE SWAIM, EXECUTIVE DIRECTOR
JOHN LOUNSBURY, SENIOR EDITOR
MARY MITCHELL, COPY EDITOR/
    DESIGNER

PMSA

CELINE MATZ, EXECUTIVE DIRECTOR
DONNA MILANOVICH, PRESIDENT
ROBERT DAVID, DIRECTOR OF
    RESEARCH/PUBLICATIONS

Library of Congress Cataloging-in-Publication Data

Moving forward from the past: early writings and current reflections
    of middle school founders / Robert David, editor.
        p.   cm.
    Includes bibliographical references.
    ISBN 1-56090-154-3 (pbk)
    1. Middle school education--United States--Philosophy. 2. Middle
schools--United States.   I. David, Robert J.   II. National Middle
School Association.   III. Pennsylvania Middle School Association.
LB1623.5. M68   1998   98-19634
373.236'0973--dc21   CIP

To **William M. Alexander**

The Father of the Middle School

1912-1996

Contents

Conrad F. Toepfer, Jr.

Gordon F. Vars

Acknowledgements

The editor wishes to thank all those who contributed to this historical work. Many people were involved in the initial phases and provided guidance throughout the completion of the text. It is especially fitting to thank Drs. Alexander, Eichhorn, Lounsbury, Toepfer, and Vars for permitting their works to be used, for offering guidance during the review process, and for preparing a reflection piece. Special thanks to Kenneth McEwin who assisted in the selection of titles and wrote a reflection on Dr. Alexander's work.

It is also appropriate to acknowledge Mary Monsour, Assistant Principal, Peters Township Middle School, for suggestions made during development of the text and proofreading, and Georgann Helman, Secretary, J.E. Harrison Middle School, for her tireless efforts to provide focus when needed. Finally, I want to thank the Executive Board of Pennsylvania Middle School Association for their ongoing support and vision in promoting middle level education.

—RD

Editor's Introduction

There have been many attempts over the years to provide sound programs and developmentally appropriate learning activities for students. Educators have grappled with the question, "How do we meet the unique needs of individual learners at various grade levels?" Schools generally were configured to combine age groups that were presumably developmentally alike: elementary for children and secondary for adolescents. Gradually, however, educators realized that two levels were not adequate. A middle unit was needed to address the distinctive needs of *young* adolescents.

The junior high school attempted to bridge the gap between the two levels. However, as a downward extension of the high school, the junior high failed to serve middle level learners appropriately. There were few, if any, specific programs instituted to meet young adolescents' needs. Instructional strategies and activities were not created with the developmental needs of these young students in mind. Educators had forgotten the importance of those students "in the middle." Thus, the middle school movement was born.

The middle school concept did not spring from sterile, educational thought. It was the result of the work of dedicated and inspired leaders who recognized that traditional secondary practices did not meet the needs of emerging adolescents. William Alexander, Donald Eichhorn, John Lounsbury, Conrad Toepfer, and Gordon Vars, identified as founding fathers of middle level education in the Founders Series,* had the vision and determination to create a new and powerful educational reform effort for the 11- to 14-year-old child. Each, in his own way, understood the limitations of the junior high school. Each focused on a vision regarding the programming and educational needs of the young adolescent. And they articulated a philosophy born out of the awareness that the middle level learner is a unique individual with special needs that call for a distinctive educational program.

This collection of writings and speeches chronicles the early thinking of these five visionaries. Each author selected three or four articles from his earlier publications or presentations. The pieces were written or spoken in the years between 1956 and 1977. Then each provided a "reflection" piece. These fresh articles are particularly interesting and valuable. Developed independently without guidelines, they range from Eichhorn's informative historical review of the movement to Toepfer's passionate call for moral education. In toto, this collection provides a marvelous perspective on middle level educational development.

The National Middle School Association and the Pennsylvania Middle School Association are pleased to join in bringing this important work to the profession. A representative of each association has provided a foreword that further sets the stage for the remainder of the volume. It is being highlighted in Denver as a part of the celebration of NMSA's 25th anniversary.

This text is an inspiration for those of us who have become second generation middle school educators. While others only watched and complained about the neglected educational needs of the preadolescent, these leaders accepted the challenge and forged a new educational reform. To Drs. Alexander, Eichhorn, Lounsbury, Toepfer, and Vars we are most indebted.

Bob David
Associate Professor
California University of Pennsylvania

* Articles describing the lives and contributions of these individuals were carried in the *Middle School Journal* as "The Founders Series." The idea was conceived by journal editor Tom Dickinson who enlisted Tom Erb to serve as coordinator for the series. It consisted of the following articles:
   "William M. Alexander: Father of the American Middle School,"
        by C. Kenneth McEwin, May 1992, pp. 32-38.
   "Donald H. Eichhorn: Pioneer in Inventing Schools for Transescents,"
        by Judith Allen Brough, March 1994, pp. 18-22.
   "John H. Lounsbury: Conscience of the Middle School Movement,"
        by J. Howard Johnston, November 1992, pp. 45-50.
   "Conrad F. Toepfer, Jr.: The Jazz Man of Middle Level Education,"
        by Sherrel K. Bergmann, January 1994, pp. 25-28.
   "Gordon F. Vars: The Heart and Soul of Core Curriculum,"
        by Daniel Dyer, January 1993, pp. 31-38.

Foreword

As I write this foreword I feel like my professional life has come full circle. Thirty-plus years ago, when completing a doctorate in curriculum and instruction, I was introduced to the new (at the time) middle school movement in the United States. My interests in the junior high school and young adolescents were already well established because of prior teaching experience, and I had planned to focus on them in my doctoral research. However, little did I know the exciting world that was about to open when my advisor, the late Maurice McGlasson at Indiana University, guided me to the writings of the pioneers featured in this volume.

The middle school ideas and concepts William M. Alexander, Donald H. Eichhorn, John H. Lounsbury, Conrad F. Toepfer, Jr., and Gordon F. Vars wrote about were revolutionary because they challenged the traditional junior high school that I thought I understood and believed in. I read and reread their works – many of them featured in this volume – discussed them with other educators, and wrote about them. I visited some of the schools that had been designed or restructured as middle schools along the lines they recommended. My doctoral dissertation compared traditional junior high schools with new middle schools. In the process, I was transformed to a new way of thinking about educating young adolescents that has defined my educational career ever since. Of much greater importance, their work spawned an educational revolution.

The middle school movement of the past four decades has been one of the great watersheds of American educational history. Beginning from early experiments that many critics dismissed as another fad of the 1960s, middle level schools have endured and flourished. The important retrospective study published by the National Middle School Association in 1996, *America's Middle Schools: Practices and Progress – A 25 Year Perspective,* chronicled the lasting conceptual and organizational strength and vitality of middle level education.

The ideas and challenges issued by the authors whose works you will read in this volume provided the visionary yeast that made it all happen. And they're timeless. Read them historically, but also read them in the context of education today. Many of the issues they addressed are still with us and can be helped by a reexamination of their practical guidelines and advice. Examine some of the topics; they're just as relevant today as when they were written: curriculum content, teacher preparation, grade organization, learner characteristics and needs, pupil grouping, articulation of learning experiences.

It is quite fitting that the National Middle School Association has chosen to co-publish the historic masterpieces of these trailblazers on the occasion of its 25th anniversary celebration in Denver, Colorado, in 1998. Without them and the movement they helped initiate, NMSA might not exist.

The men of this volume have been my professional heroes. I have had the esteemed privilege of knowing each of them personally and have had the good fortune to work closely with some of them. With the exception of the late Bill Alexander, who passed away two years ago, they still serve selflessly as middle level writers, editors, speakers, and consultants. Not content with the successes of the past or the status quo, they continue to extend ideas and challenges to keep middle level schools on the cutting edge in the new millennium. Be ready to be energized and challenged as you read these classics.

— **Tom Gatewood,**
Director, Education Programs,
Northern Virginia Center, Virginia Tech

Foreword

As I sit to write a foreword to this book, I am personally overwhelmed by the opportunity to comment in any way on the works of the scholars contained herein. Through my affiliation with and work for the Pennsylvania Middle School Association and the National Middle School Association, I have treasured the opportunity for contact with educators the caliber of William M. Alexander, Donald H. Eichhorn, John H. Lounsbury, Conrad F. Toepfer, Jr., and Gordon F. Vars – the founding fathers of middle level education. I have been particularly fortunate to have had a personal and professional relationship with Donald H. Eichhorn. A mentor and a friend, Don has helped me to formulate my personal philosophy of middle level education. As a member of my dissertation committee, Don provided expert advice and guidance as I worked to develop evaluation procedures and assessment instruments for a middle level program.

The pioneering work of these men in middle level education has enabled practitioners to plan and implement developmentally appropriate learning environments for ten to fourteen year olds. The scope of their impact extends not only nationally but internationally as well. One might legitimately ask, "Why explore the historical works of our founding fathers?" We are reminded by the great statesman Winston Churchill that, "The farther back you can look, the farther forward you are likely to see." This statement rings clearly true for the insights and writings of these men. The vision they have bequeathed to us is as viable today as when they first formulated their ideas forty years ago.

The historical perspective of the middle level movement is best served by investigating early efforts at the turn of the century to reorganize secondary education by designing a school program that would meet the unique needs of the young adolescent. In the 1920s, the earliest proponents of the junior high school espoused the need for schools to address the characteristics of the preadolescent. Over the years the recommendations of those early leaders were lost as the junior high school eventually mirrored the high school model, rarely serving well the children that it was originally designed to accommodate. The work of the middle level founding fathers, Alexander, Eichhorn, Lounsbury, Toepfer, and Vars, helped educators and public officials to redefine an appropriate educational program for preadolescents and once again focus on the middle level learner. They spoke and wrote eloquently of developmentally appropriate practices that addressed the physical, intellectual, social, and emotional characteristics of the learner.

Thanks to their commitment and their work, the status of middle level education has been elevated to its rightful place in the K through 12 continuum, and we shall never return to our former thinking. As Oliver Wendell Holmes so aptly stated:

> The MIND,
> once expanded to the dimensions of a larger idea,
> NEVER returns to its original size.

Educators and young adolescents everywhere thank you – our founding fathers.

Donna K. Milanovich
President
Pennsylvania Middle School Association

I

William M. Alexander

William Alexander knew about and endorsed enthusiastically this project. However, his failing health and ultimate death in August of 1996 prevented his taking part in preparing this volume. As his professional colleague and good friend, I agreed to assist in the selection of articles and in preparing a reflection piece.

The first selection is the presentation that really launched, in many respects, the middle school movement. In it Dr. Alexander first used the term *middle school* and what this alternative-to-the-junior-high-school would be like. Three years later he spoke at an early, if not the first conference on the middle school. This presentation is the second piece to be included. The last article was published in the **Phi Delta Kappan** in 1969. It reports the survey conducted by Dr. Alexander that became the benchmark from which the growth of middle schools has been charted.

— C. Kenneth McEwin

WILLIAM M. ALEXANDER

The Junior High School: A Changing View

A presentation made in the summer of 1963 at Cornell University

It is not my task to summarize or seek to interpret what has gone before. Rather, Professor Johnson asked me to look forward with you, attempting to "identify the features of the junior high school that seem to be undergoing change and those which seem to endure." And so, I shall start out with a review of four characteristics of the junior high school which have been somewhat continuously sought and, to varying degrees, attained. Of these characteristics, I would also ask: Should they continue, and why or why not?

Then I shall describe three other characteristics which many of us seek in the middle school of the future, and close my presentation with some hypotheses as to a partial, tentative model of this new middle school we need.

Characteristics of the junior high school which continue

From its beginnings, the junior high school has sought to be a transitional or bridge institution between the elementary and the high school. This characteristic has been vigorously questioned both as to its appropriateness and its actual development.

As to appropriateness, certainly there is need to ease the transition of learners from childhood to adolescence. This type of transition function is more relevant to my second characteristic, however. Also, as long as the program and organization of the elementary schools differed sharply, there was, and is, real need for a bridge between the self-contained classroom of the elementary school with its broad and flexible units of work and the departmentalized program of the high school with its relatively greater emphasis on subjects and specialization. These differences are becoming much less sharp, however, as subjects are once again being pushed downward, as departmentalization of various sorts is again spreading in the elementary grades, and as vertical curriculum planning in the major subjects makes more progress. That is, there are the distinct signs, commented on in Professor Broudy's paper and elsewhere, that the differences between the last years of the elementary school and the first ones of the high school – junior, senior, 4-year, or 6-year – are not nearly so severe and distinct as a decade ago, or indeed as many feel they should be.

However needed a transition is between the elementary and the high school, there are grave doubts as to the functioning of the junior high school in this regard. It is an interesting commentary on this function of the entire junior high school that after these schools had been widely established, a return from their departmentalized organization, à la the high school, was sought in the block-time or core program. The chief justification of this program is to ease the transition from elementary to junior high school – a clear admission that the usually departmentalized program and organization of the junior high school tended to defeat the transitional function. Other evidence abounds that the "junior" high school has typically been a secondary school following the 4-year high school model rather than being an in-between school, bridging a gap between elementary and secondary education. As Professor Johnson pointed out in his *Saturday Review* article, the transition that was originally of greatest concern was that of making "the academic initiation at grade nine easier for pupils" rather than the transition from grade six to seven or the one represented by pubescence. The general adoption by junior high schools of the schedule, the activity program, and the organization of the high school attests to the dominance of the idea that the bridge was fundamentally a vestibule added at the front door of the high school.

Thus, there is a major question as to whether the junior high school as it now exists should defend its existence on the transitional basis. Indeed we doubt whether any institution can have real purpose and vitality if its role is subordinated either to the separate institutions it bridges or the one for which it serves a preparatory function. I would vote for elimination of the separateness of current elementary, junior and senior high schools, with the resulting need for bridges, and for instead a 12- to 14-year institution, with three levels in its vertical structure, each of which has a program and organization appropriate to its place in a sequential educational pattern. Thus, there would be a lower, middle, and upper level, or a primary, middle, and high school.

Despite the criticisms already made here and elsewhere, we should affirm the belief that the junior high school, even as a "junior" institution, has provided for some needs of the preadolescent, certainly better than in the narrower program of the 8-grade elementary school or of the more regimented one of the high school. In good junior high schools, boys and girls have had more of the freedom of movement they need, more appropriate health and physical education, more chances to participate in planning and managing their own activities, more resources for help on their problems of growing up, and more opportunities to explore new interests and to develop new aspirations. All of these features we would definitely continue in the middle school of the future.

A third continuing characteristic of the junior high school has been its program of exploratory experiences. Once a pre-vocational education function, exploration has been broadened to include a wider variety of possible interests. There seems little disagreement that the youngster of twelve and above needs many and varied opportunities to identify and/or deepen worthwhile interests, and all of us would applaud what junior high schools have done to this end. However, the recent pressures on schools to give greater emphasis to the academic subject may be curtailing the exploratory feature. Earlier languages, more mathematics and science, more homework, may mean for many pupils less time and energy for the fine arts, for homemaking and industrial arts, and for such special interests as dramatics, journalism, musical performance, scouting, camping outside jobs, and general reading.

Furthermore, many view the 6, 9, 12, or even 18-weeks elective courses in grades 8 and 9 as inadequate exploration. In some areas these may be the only possibilities, but we wonder if different scheduling and a different relationship of subjects and activities might facilitate many independent experiences and projects developing either from the classroom, the counseling situation, the activity program, or just from the pupil's expressed interest? Could the middle school give more emphasis to independent study and activity as an aid to the transition from childhood to adolescence? Perhaps we need more special interest centers competently supervised and operated on a flexible time basis in which children can get guidance and experience in such varied activities as reading, acting, writing, painting, ceramics, mechanics of the automobile and home, typing, photography, and personal grooming and many others.

The fourth characteristic of the junior high school is one all support – continued general education. Probably most of us would heartily agree with our hosts here at Cornell that there is great need to underline the intellectual growth phase of this program. Certainly curriculum planning at the junior high school level has been no more successful than elsewhere, perhaps less so, in defining the scope and sequence of an adequate general education. Possibly the difficulty has lain in part in the feeling that the subjects in "junior" high school must be very different from the elementary school, although repetition has continued. My own view is that the junior high school break has unwittingly hastened the disrespect for intellectual activity too common among adolescents. Has the "junior" high school, with its imitation of the high school activity and social programs, hastened and fixed more firmly the ideals of athletic prowess (boys) and popularity (girls) over academic brilliance as reported in Coleman's study of *The Adolescent Society*?

Continued general education in the junior high school must indeed give a new emphasis to intellectual development. This it must do, I believe, by more skillful teaching and more careful curriculum planning, rather than by more, or even continued, pressures on grades, and preparation for high school and college.

Other characteristics to be sought in the middle school

Several factors point to the need for a vigorous attempt in the middle school to focus on the individualization of instruction. Although the primary school certainly pays attention to individual differences, its program is most of all one of integration of young children into accepted patterns of communication and social behavior. Habits of conformity are well-enough developed in most 10 to 12 year-olds to indicate a need for opening up opportunities for individual deviations of a wholesome and promising variety.

I was impressed by Dr. Paul Torrance's report recently of studies in youngsters' creative behavior that showed a decided slump for many children beginning about the fourth grade. Is our emphasis on the group and on conformity in the middle grades contributing to the inhibition of creative ideas and activities?

We are all familiar, too, with the characteristic resistance to schools and schooling which begins to be expressed even in the third and fourth grades. Whether real or fancied, the apparent disposition of many children to discount educational purposes and programs reflects inadequate motivation to intellectual achievement. It is at this level, too, that underachievement is first readily identified. The potential dropout is noted, and the need for individual help and stimulation weights heavily on the conscientious, sympathetic teacher.

Ability grouping and programs for special groups may be only hiding the needs of the individual in the group. Whether he be the potential artist, or dropout, the intellectually stimulated or unmotivated, Johnny needs all the attention he can get from a teacher who knows him well and respects his individuality.

To help in individualization, the middle school needs to provide adequate diagnostic and guidance services. It also needs to permit teachers to work individually with children and their parents. All of the other known aids to individualization – for example, a variety of learning resources, time and place for independent study, self-evaluation devices, individual projects, opportunities for varied pupil roles in classroom and school organizations – should be abundant in the middle school years.

A related second characteristic to be sought in the middle school of the future is a flexible curriculum, permitting and indeed aiding pupils to progress at different rates and to different depths. Although the requirements of continued general education make mandatory some beginning points and goals in the basic curriculum fields, minimum grade standards subject by subject can defeat the aims of intellectual development. Programmed instructional materials in mathematics and language arts may help to pace an individual's learning progress. Unit-of-work approaches in social studies and science can provide differentiated tasks for learners. In matters of performance, individuals can be challenged to seek their own level of attainment in playing an instrument, using paints and easels, or hitting a softball.

But even greater flexibility must come through a reconsideration of classroom organization and procedure. The middle grades seem none too early to initiate some pupils into plans of curriculum differentiation which provide for certain ones to work on reading improvement in a reading center, while some classmates are reading in the classroom under their teacher's guidance, and still others are using the library for more challenging materials. Or a few pupils may be working with a speech teacher, others preparing a dramatic presentation, and others in the language laboratory learning a modern foreign language.

In all studies continued attention would be given to the learning process itself. The teacher demonstrates how sources are used to get answers to real questions, and pupils apply the procedures to questions they investigate. Reference books, textbooks, interviews, current newspapers and magazines, and other sources are fully utilized as methods of inquiry; they replace methods of memorization as the focal points of teaching and learning. Although facts are kept central, fact-finding rather than fact-memorizing and reciting is emphasized in the flexible curriculum of essential learning processes instead of minimum essentials of definitions, dates, and details in general. The curriculum which should be characteristic of the middle school must reflect such an educational belief as was stated by the Winnetka Public Schools as their number one objective in a recent publication of *Beliefs and Objectives*, under the heading of "Give Primary and Unremitting Devotion to Intellectual Growth." The statement in part is as follows:

> Intellectual growth means much more than an increasing competence in the academic content of the curriculum. We must endeavor to stimulate in the child a love for learning, an attitude of inquiry, a passion for truth and beauty, a questioning mind. The learning of right answers is not enough ...beyond answers alone, we must help

children ask right questions, and discover their answers through creative thinking, reasoning, judging, and understanding. We must help children know that learning is its own reward, uncluttered by momentary symbolic rewards for accomplishments or penalties for failures.

Learning can best flourish when teachers, supported by adequate materials, create a climate in which children are genuinely desirous of learning. It will flourish when children become, through the teacher's stimulation, self-motivated, knowing that learning is necessary and important, and why they are engaged upon it. And it behooves us to be sure that it is necessary and important. Conclusions, values, solutions to problems are not taught ...they are learned, created, possessed internally by the child, having been excited by the teacher, and having been led by the teacher to the place where the answers might be found.

A final, and somewhat summarizing, characteristic to be sought in the middle school is an emphasis on values. In the upper or high school boys and girls are beset by conflicts in value systems. In the early school years, these conflicts were less real or absent. Between the primary and later years is a real opportunity for the school to provide leadership in fixing values which will survive the perils ahead. As boys and girls are challenged in the middle grades to assume responsibility for their own actions, to respect each other and the adults with whom they associate, and to distinguish right from wrong, truth from falsehood, they can grow to a real independence.

Every class, every pupil-teacher conversation, every school activity is a setting for the development of values. The responsiveness of the older children and preadolescents makes the middle grades an especially desirable level for a continuing emphasis on this aspect of education.

A tentative model for the new middle school

The "changing view" I have seen and reflected here is by now obvious to you as a view of a middle unit in a vertically planned educational system. This unit or school may comprise what is now called the junior high school; however, this unit is really a third quarter, too much like the final quarter. Perhaps it will be the grade 6-8 unit, now growing in popularity. I would personally prefer to see it as near a middle unit as possible, namely, what now constitutes grades 5-8.

Experimentation with a new middle school (best developed in new building programs, although it could be accomplished by modifying present junior high school structures), should serve several purposes, it is suggested:

1. It would give this unit a status of its own, rather than a "junior" classification.

2. It would facilitate the introduction in grades 5 and 6 of some specialization and team teaching in staffing patterns.

3. It would also facilitate the reorganization of teacher education sorely needed to provide teachers competent for the middle school; since existing patterns of neither elementary nor secondary teacher training would suffice, a new pattern would have to be developed.

4. A clearly defined middle unit should more easily have the other characteristics already described as desirable, than the typical junior high school: (a) a well-articulated 12- to 14-year system of education; (b) preparation for, even transition to, adolescence; (c) continued general education; and (d) abundant opportunities for exploration of interests, individualization of instruction, a flexible curriculum, and emphasis on values.

I hope that the suggestions made here do not amount to the "major surgery" Dr. Johnson mentioned in his *Saturday Review* article as being often prescribed by critics; he stated that these proposals generally had "about as much chance of being pulled off as has the abolition of the income tax." I hope the specifics of this tentative model now proposed may get some further consideration and tried out as applicable, perhaps in a few complete experimental units.

I. The program might have these phases:

A. Learning skills: reading, writing, speaking, listening,

computation skills continued from the elementary school, with new emphases on use of library tools and self-teaching devices.

B. Other common learnings: literature, social studies, languages, mathematics, science, and fine arts, following a sequence of instruction in these areas planned for grades K-12.

C. Personal development: health, and physical education geared to the 10-14 year old; individually planned experiences in foreign languages, typing, fine and practical arts, and remedial basic skills; other exploratory experiences through independent study and a program of special interest activities and student-managed enterprises; close relationship with a counselor-teacher throughout the middle school; and adequate diagnostic tests, parent conferences, and other data sources for counseling.

II. The organization of the middle school might include these arrangements:

A. A team of three to five teachers (one or two especially competent in language arts and social studies, one or two in science and mathematics, and one in fine arts and/or languages) could be assigned to each group of 75 to 150 pupils, organized either on a single grade or multigrade basis. These teachers would be responsible for about two-thirds of the instruction of these pupils, on a team basis according to such plans as are appropriate to curriculum goals, teacher competencies, and school organization.

B. Each pupil would be a member of a small homeroom group, which would be assigned to one of the team members for counseling and individual scheduling for special programs.

C. Each pupil would participate daily in a program of health and physical education directed by a specialist in this area.

D. Such special instructional and/or laboratory centers as the following would be available for several purposes, with each center manned by a teacher competent in individualized instruction: reading; writing; speech; mathematics; library; foreign languages; typing; music; art; industrial arts; home economics; dramatics. Pupils would be scheduled for work in these centers on an individualized basis for both short-term and long-term instruction as needed.

E. The basic instructional units (75 to 150 pupils) and the homeroom groups (3 to 5 in each unit) would be organized on a heterogeneous basis as to ability. The teaching team might arrange some instruction in basic skills by groups determined for this purpose according to status in the skills concerned.

III. Personnel arrangements might include:

A. A principal whose major duties involve the coordination of basic instructional units and special instructional centers, and leadership in curriculum planning and evaluation activities.

B. An assistant principal (assuming 500 or more pupils) to manage supporting administrative and auxiliary school services and to supervise record-keeping, clerical, and fiscal operations.

C. Special staff positions: curriculum research and evaluation, psychological services, health services, etc.

D. Classification of teachers as either (1) homeroom or (2) special center, there being no differential in status or salary due to this classification.

E. Homeroom teachers would work with pupils about two-thirds of their scheduled time and have one-third available for team planning, individual preparation, and parent conferences. Special center teachers would have an appropriate period available daily for individual preparation and conferences with teach team members.

F. Employment and assignment of faculty based on:
(1) Five to six years' college training and three or more years' successful teaching experience before permanent license.

(2) For all teachers a major in their teaching field(s) through the Master's degree, with adequate professional education of a practice-oriented nature.

(3) Equivalent of a doctorate in the field of specialization for all administrative and special staff positions.

(4) Salary schedule provisions for recognition of superior training and performance. ▶

Program and Organization of a Five Through Eight Middle School

Presentation at the Mt. Kisko Conference, 1966

I was, of course, very pleased and delighted to have an opportunity to be here in your New York State, and particularly at this conference on the middle school. As one who, in the last few years, has been raising some questions about the characteristic organization of our school system it pleases and interests me to know that so many institutions and so many school people are responding with questions of their own – that they are interested to take a look once again at the continuity of education from school entrance to school termination and to think about what is the most appropriate program for different levels of schooling.

I would like to make it clear that in coming to talk with you, I really have no ax to grind, nor program to promote. I have some considerable interest in this matter and I think possibly it is appropriate to take a little while to tell you what these interests are and why they are. I am not at all certain of any categorical answer to the question of what school really should bridge the elementary school and the high school. As a matter of fact, may I point out to you that throughout our educational history, many communities have had no in-between school at all.

It has been only about 50 years since our first junior high school was opened, and already this institution has become a very large sector of our educational establishment. During these past 50 years, increasing need has been felt for some kind of school to bridge the elementary school and the high school. And so I think I might appropriately entitle what I have to talk to you about, "a school to bridge elementary and high school," or "to bridge childhood and adolescence." I could not help reflecting, as I flew in here last evening, on the changes that have occurred with regard to this question in the last three years. It was exactly three years ago this month that I flew to Cornell University to address a conference sponsored by the junior high school group there on "The Changing Junior High School." At that time I talked about the desirability as I saw it, of some reorganization of the junior high school into a middle school. I remember that at the conclusion of that conference, two people spoke to me about organizations that were occurring in their district. Now there may have been more in New York State, but I only learned at that time about a couple. It was the following fall of course, that the committee in New York released the report recommending a 4-4-4 type organization for somewhat different reasons. This timing was sheer coincidence, for I knew nothing of that committee report, and I am sure the committee knew nothing of my speech. But during these three years that have elapsed, there has been quite a movement away from the 6-3-3 organization in your state and in other states, particularly in this section of the country. I know today when we talk about a middle school organization, the idea is not quite so novel, and there are more persons with experience, or interest in the school. My fear is, and I say this quite deliberately, that we may be going into too much of a bandwagon-type movement without the careful reflections, discussions, planning and organization needed to have a better school program.

And so it is significant that you people have come together this summer to reflect about what kind of school program and organization you need. Three years ago when I talked for the first time in my experience on the need for reorganization of the junior high school, again today when I talk to somewhat the same topic but in a somewhat different context, I am motivated primarily by three reasons. I think I would like to explain these educational reasons because I am not suggesting that a reorganization is needed to solve building, enrollment, or desegregation problems, or any of the other problems that are not really related to the educational program itself, regardless of how important they may otherwise be.

My first reason lies in a very strong belief, shared I am sure by everyone here, certainly by the majority of American educators, that we must have a continuous program that takes youngsters from school entry to school termination, and in these years, helps each boy and girl move somewhat gradually from dependence in his learning activities, to independence. If I could have my wishes, and I think I speak for all of you, I would want every youngster who graduated from an American high school to have become so well educated during these years of progress from the first grade or kindergarten or the pre-primary grade, wherever we pick him up, that he is now able, really and truly to continue his own education. The one fact that seems inescapably clear, as we look towards the last third of the twentieth century in America, is that the individual who succeeds, socially and personally, will be the individual who is able to continue learning on his own. There are certain realities of the present and certain probabilities of the future that do make ours a learning society in which a growing number of individuals will be spending more and more of their lifetime in a highly active, highly motivated pursuit of learning.

I point to three factors. First, there is a strong and wonderful movement, with all of its problems, toward a new recognition of the rights of each individual in our society, including the right to the best opportunities possible to continue learning on his own. Some of our new educational programs show a new concern for the culturally deprived and many other members of our society. And we may be, for the first time, putting into educational action a very beautiful philosophy of education of living that is summed up for me in a very brief quote from Goethe: "If you treat an individual as he is, he will stay as he is, but if you treat him as he ought to be and could be, he will become what he ought to be and could be." I believe we are attempting, these days in education, more satisfactorily and more adequately, despite all the problems involved, to treat individuals more as they ought to be and could be rather than as they are. And as we do this, we are helping these learners move into their full status and place in the learning society of our country.

The second fact that points to the necessity of developing each individual to the point where he will learn on his own, is the familiar constellation of facts which we loosely call the knowledge revolution or the knowledge explosion. I won't bore you with all the statistics, for you and I have only to review our own lifetime to be impressed with the rapidity of change and with the added expansion of knowledge. It is impressive to recognize that on the average every ten minutes some new invention is patented by the U.S. government, and that every day 2,000 pages of new information are released by the presses of research organizations, business, industry, and government. It is inescapably clear that the growing body of knowledge is such that we cannot possibly expect to teach children all they need to know – the most we can do is to teach them what they need to know in order to learn what they need to know when they need it.

And the third fact that points to the necessity of training people to learn on their own is that of occupational change and mobility. We are told that the typical youngster now in school will engage in three different work careers; because of the changes in our society and in occupational patterns, we cannot possibly expect to train the average youngster while in school even for his first career. We can merely get him pointed to one or more careers, and expect him to be able to carry on this own training and retraining thereafter with the aid of schools, industrial training programs, military programs, and university professional schools.

So I emphasize that today there is need for a new educational program and organization to provide more continuity in education – a continuity which will help every student to be capable of learning on his own by the time he completes school. The second reason that I lean toward a new school organization has to do with the facts of human development about which you heard this morning. To me they suggest that any type of school organization must be highly flexible. It must encourage each individual to work up to his own capacity without artificial barriers between school levels and school buildings. Everything we are able to put together in our growing body of knowledge about individual growth and development points to the wide diversity of individuals, to the great differences in aspirations and capacities of the individuals we teach.

Let me just mention a few of these facts. For example, when intelligence is measured and converted into age units, the range among the first graders who will enter your schools this September will be about four years. Actually in a random population 96 out of 100 children will vary from 4 to 8 years mentally, with 2 below 4, and 2 above 8. We also know that this range of ability will widen as they continue in school so that by the time these children have reached the 8th grade, you may expect a range of from 9 to 10 years in their ability. We also know that similar differences are found in their achievement in the various subjects. By the 7th grade, we can confidently expect a range between individuals of some 8 years in their achievement in the different subject fields. Furthermore, the range of achievement in various subjects by the same individual also may be great. To the extent that the range of intellectual differences among children is an argument for nongradedness (and it is the main argument, of course), there is much more basis for nongradedness in the middle years than in the primary ones. But this is not the most obvious type of difference in the middle school years. It is the phenomenon of puberty which begins to appear in these years that most sharply accentuates differences among individuals. Some girls achieve menarche in grade 5, although a few girls and more boys will not reach this stage until the high school years. Although the differences between the sexes is pronounced, there are also marked differences as to the time of attainment of puberty within the same sex. And so children of ages 10 to 14 exhibit very marked differences in their physical, social, and emotional development. By age 15, about 85% of the population have become pubescent, and a relative degree of homogeneity related to this factor is evident as adolescents enter grade 9.

The wide range of differences among children between childhood and adolescence points to the necessity for a flexible type of school organization rather than one that is fixed and sacred.

The third group of factors which lead me to conclude that some organization other than the 6-3-3 organization, as we know it, may be better, are certain practices characteristic of this now traditional organization. It simply does not seem to have provided well enough the continuity that we need in education and it tends to be out of joint with today's levels of human growth and development.

Any educational organization serving children from ages 5 or 6 to about 18, ought to have three fairly distinct levels. One would be the level of childhood education which we have thought of as the elementary school. At the other extreme is adolescent education which we have usually defined as the job of the high school. In between childhood and adolescence, there is the need for a third level of education which would be middle school education or education of the in-between group: the older child, the preadolescent, and the early adolescent.

When we examine the programs characteristic of the 6-3-3 plan, I think we definitely see some flaws. First, looking at the junior high school, it was, of course, established back in 1910 as a school to serve the in-betweens; it was to be a transitional school, from elementary to high school. But other reasons for the junior high school became more compelling: to save time, to eliminate the inefficiency of the 8th grade of the old 8-4 plan, to meet the problem of population expansion in cities after World War I. What seems to have happened with the junior high school organization is that a unique program for in-betweener's was overshadowed by a program for adolescents. The junior came to look too much like the senior high departmentalization, and an activity program and a social program for adolescents got established. The needs of the older children dominated the program and made it too mature and sophisticated a program for those who are still in between childhood and adolescence.

In looking at the elementary school I find as serious a problem as I do in the junior high school. The elementary school, as we know it, characteristically has placed a great emphasis on the role of the individual teacher as the guide, the counselor, and the teacher on a self-contained classroom basis for all of the children in his or her room. This type of organization is excellent, so it seems, for early childhood and childhood up to age 10 or 11. But when you look at this organization in the face of increasing specialization of knowledge, with the increasing need for teachers to be thoroughly abreast of the special fields in which they teach, and when you look at it in terms of these earlier maturing youngsters who do need more challenge in their school studies, it is doubtful whether the self-contained organization can really endure. Is it possible, is it feasible, is it even desirable, for a 5th or 6th grade teacher to deal adequately with all of the subjects of the curriculum? Now of course, one answer is to departmentalize the elementary school. But this brings into the elementary school the same faults of the junior high school

organization, and I do not for one moment propose departmentalization as the way to organize and instruct a middle school.

When we examine the 6-3-3 plan further, we also have to recognize that the 9th grade has never been firmly established as a junior
high school year. Even though it has been housed in the junior high
school, it has been accounted for as a senior high school grade.
Schools have been bound by state education department and
accreditation association regulations, even by the statistical systems
of the United States Office of Education, to identify the 9th grade as
a high school grade. Frequently out of joint with the 7th and 8th
grades, or causing the 7th and 8th grades to be put on the same
Carnegie unit system, the 9th grade has frequently been a misfit in
junior high.

Now recognizing that most 9th graders are fully adolescent, is it
not desirable to firmly fix the 9th grade back in the high school
where it has tended to be anyway and to have a well-rounded 4-
year high school unit?

Now I want to talk about some of the things we have provided in
the junior high schools that should be retained in the middle
school. Before I do this, let me emphasize that in this age of educational innovation and experimentation, the middle school organization seems to offer an excellent opportunity for research on an
educational program designed to increase rather than stifle intellectual curiosity and endeavor. It was this I think that led Paul
Woodring last fall, in the *Saturday Review*, to comment most
favorably on the intermediate school. In fact I thought he went a
little far out when he said the 6-3-3 plan was definitely passing out
of existence – after all, there are still some 6,500 junior high schools
in the United States. But his reason for emphasizing the possibilities
of what he called the "intermediate school," or the middle school,
was that it offered abundant opportunities for new staffing patterns
including the use of team teaching, for the use of programmed
learning, independent study, and new course contents and, as a
necessity, the development of a new kind of teacher education at
this level.

I think we may work, as we look into the opportunities for the
junior high school, to be certain that we do more than simply try to

get on the bandwagon because of discontent with what we have. Now let me try to be more positive and suggest some guidelines for building a model middle school program – one that would retain the advantages, hopefully of the elementary school, and of the junior high school, but that basically will be a school for the age group we are talking about.

My first guideline is that this middle school should be designed to serve the needs of older children, preadolescents and early adolescents. It should be planned as a bridge school, a definite bridge from the school for childhood to the school for adolescents, not as a vestibule to the senior high school which the junior high school tends to be. Let's create a separate school able to stand on its own with definite plans and programs so as to bridge well the elementary and the high school, providing for continuity of education. We know that children in this age bracket, in the 10 or 11 to 14 year old group, need freedom of movement, opportunities for initiative, a voice in the running of their own affairs, the intellectual stimulation of working with different groups and with different teacher specialists.

I would suggest as another guideline, that this middle school organization, should make a reality of the long-held ideal of individualized instruction; that here we would definitely try to develop a learner interested in learning on his own by giving him or her a maximum of the services which would insure a liking for learning. I would have every pupil in the middle school assigned to a teacher counselor who knows him well and will work with him if at all possible and feasible throughout his years in the middle school. I would have an adequate program of diagnostic services which permits teachers to plan individual deviations from standard programs. There would be special instructional units where pupils may schedule work so that they can catch up on needed skills and so that they can branch out into further experimentation.

It is in this middle school too, that, I would place primary emphasis on the skills of continued learning. I refer to such plain, commonplace, but very important skills as reading, as reasoning, as asking questions, as writing, as problem-solving, as the use of the library, as the use of the reference tools and the intelligent use of all of the media which we have available for students' use. Teachers in these grade levels must be past masters of the guidance of pupils and the use of everything that is in a well-handled library. They must be past masters in teaching youngsters to ask questions, to formulate questions well, to get information from whatever sources are available and to test out their ideas, their hunches, their conclusions. Then too, there would be a beginning of independent study, as children are ready, and I expect that they are ready earlier than we generally start them. There would be opportunities for children on a flexible basis, free of group activity, free of class instruction, to work as individuals on many types of independent study.

Particularly it is in the middle school that there is needed a rich program of exploratory experiences. I think in sizing up the junior high school against its predecessor, the 8-grade elementary school, that obviously the greatest contribution made by the junior high school was the introduction of the various types of exploratory experiences. These may be less available now as a greater insistence is placed on a fuller program of academic type work.

In this middle school, there ought to be special interest studies, competently supervised, competently operated on a flexible kind of basis. These services should provide individualized instruction in each curricular area, and also in such varied activities as reading, acting, ceramics, photography, personal grooming, and also all of arts that we can possibly arrange for and afford to support. I would particularly emphasize, in the middle school, a program of health and physical education. This is desired especially for boys and girls of the middle school years, to include direct instruction in personal hygiene combined with regular participation in fitness activities, special group games, carry-over sports activities, with adequate facilities and specialized supervision for a wide range of individuals, including those needing correctional and remedial programs.

I think that most of all in these middle schools, we would do what we find always difficult, and that is to place a very deep and distinct emphasis on values. The middle school serves years which precede the full onslaught of the temptations of adolescence. These years comprise a uniquely advantageous time for helping children to formulate values of their own; to organize and question their practice in school, their behaviors, the social attitudes they encounter, the group behavior which they see. This is the opportunity for the teacher-counselor who is working very closely with a group of youngsters throughout their days in school. The object would be to get to know them so well, so personally, so intimately, that there may be steady dialogue among individual pupils and with their teacher for the basis of the judgments that the pupils reach.

Now as to the organization and the program of this middle school related to these guidelines noted: I would like to see a program set up on a three-phase basis, and this is just a grouping for convenience. First of all, I would like to emphasize the phase of basic skills and the continuation of instruction in the learning process itself. This phase might be largely on an individualized basis using some programmed instruction, with competent personnel in charge of reading skills and other centers.

Secondly, as an important phase of this program, the general studies area comprising primarily the basic academic subjects as we know them of the social studies, mathematics, language arts, and science. Here there would be a very carefully developed sequential program of studies tied into the elementary school at one end and the high school at the other with full opportunity for children to move backward and forward in this program.

Thirdly, there would certainly be the personal development aspect of the program, which would include the special programs of remedial work, independent study, and various exploratory experiences.

Each pupil would be scheduled into all three phases each year. Ideally the arrangements would add up to a nongraded organization in which each pupil would be free to move in terms of his own ability. He would not be expected to progress at the same rate nor to the same depth as any other pupil. He would not be expected to be at the same grade level in all of his studies. His program and his progress would be cooperatively planned with his homeroom teacher. I think the instructional unit of this school would be the individual. The focus would be on a program of educational diagnosis and curriculum and instruction for the individual as he comes in his later childhood from an elementary school, and as he is maturing to become the increasingly independent learner who should move into the high school.

May I mention some possible organizational highlights? Could each middle school pupil be in a homeroom of 25 pupils who are in the same year in school, but who are otherwise a heterogeneous group? I think of the homeroom teacher with his or her group of some 25 youngsters as a person who has a specialty in some one of the basic curriculum fields, but who also has sufficient insight into the preadolescent that he or she can serve as the group counselor for this homeroom. I would see this group continuing with that teacher throughout the three or four years of the middle school, so far as it is possible, feasible, and desirable. I would see the "class" in the middle school as a group of four homerooms of about 100 pupils. Each of these four homeroom teachers would represent some specialty, one in mathematics, one in science, one in language arts, and one in social studies. These four teachers would operate as a team, a team constantly responsible for planning the basic program possible for that class of 100 students. There would be many different plans of teaching in this organization. I suspect that as children enter the middle school, for the first few weeks, maybe a good part of the first year, it would be largely a self-contained teaching plan, at least for these four basic areas. But as teachers plan together, they would begin to provide for some specialization of teaching. Thus the mathematics specialist might do more of the mathematics and there might be regrouping for this. There could be some very small group instruction and some large group instruction, too, with scheduling arranged so that each teacher shared in the work of the total class. As I see it, in a good middle school, you cannot possibly set up a schedule for a year, a semester, or even a month in advance, but the team of teachers working with their 100 or so pupils would have to make, from week to week, and sometimes from day to day, the best kind of plan possible for this group.

Basic studies or the common learning programs might comprise about two-thirds of the school day, the other one-third to be spent in special centers with specialists in charge of reading laboratories, foreign language laboratories, arts and crafts, and other laboratories.

The vertical unit, assuming you have a school of 800 or larger, could be a school within a school. There might be a unit comprising four classes of 100 each, about 400 pupils with 16 teachers in the basic areas, plus the special teachers needed. This would give the children in the little school a wider community in which to get acquainted, in which to develop new social understandings, in which to attain leadership, but not one so large as to become depersonalized.

I have already mentioned that in this organization we need especially organized centers, centers that would serve the exploratory interests and the remedial and development aspects of the school program. Pupils would not be pinned here in classes. They would be assigned to work in these centers sometimes for a short term of instruction, sometimes for a longer term.

Now let me sum up. My chief point has been that we do need for these children who are moving from childhood to adolescence, the very best educational program that can be provided. It is here that we can build true learners or we can encourage youngsters to get out of school just as quickly as possible. It is here that we can get progression or regression in learning. It is here that we can help to develop the future successful and happy individual, or we can help to create the delinquent segment of our society.

In planning the middle school program, I have suggested three features of the elementary and junior high school of today that we must retain. One is the closeness of every pupil to some one teacher, which is characteristic of the elementary school with its self-contained organization. I have substituted for that in the middle school, the idea of the homeroom teacher who would work with a group of children for a portion of each day, at least for one year. I have also suggested that we ought to hold to the gains made in the junior high school with the exploratory specializations we have provided there. Let's increase them, let's make them available earlier, to build the interests and stimulate the intellectual activity of the 5th and 6th graders. Thirdly, I suggested that we need to hold onto and improve our emphasis on the learning skills which has characterized the elementary school regrettably more than it has the junior high school.

It hardly needs to be added that moving one or two grades up from the elementary school and the present program of those grades will not create a middle school. We cannot assume that simply taking the self-contained 6th grade out of the elementary school and putting it into a new middle school, and holding onto the 7th and 8th grades on a departmentalized basis of the junior high school will create a real middle school organization. This would just place two schools under one roof. Instead this ought to be the opportunity to plan for a fundamentally different kind of organization utilizing team teaching and some aspects of a nongraded structure to provide a much richer experience for all the children.

In conclusion, I would emphasize that whatever program is experimented with ought to be truly experimental. It ought to be set up on a basis so that the question can be answered in a few years: "Was this program really better than the one we had before?"

I doubt if a school district should consider going into a middle school program without allowing at least one full year of careful planning and studying for program development and experimental design. In any event, whatever new program is introduced should be as carefully thought out, and as hopefully and as enthusiastically conducted as possible. ▶

WILLIAM M. ALEXANDER

The New School in the Middle

Published in *Phi Delta Kappan*, February, 1969

T he problems of the junior high school as the school in the middle of the school ladder have rarely if ever been put so well as in Mauritz Johnson's article titled "The School in the Middle" in *Saturday Review* of July 21, 1962. Indeed, Johnson's critique of the junior high school was a major basis of the proposal I presented at a junior high school conference headed by Mr. Johnson at Cornell University the following summer (1963). This proposal was one for a "new school in the middle," a middle school differing from prior schools bridging elementary and high schools. During the more than six years which have elapsed I have participated as a protagonist, critic, and student of the newly developing and now burgeoning middle school organizations. This article represents my gleanings of what has happened, is happening, and may yet happen with regard to the new schools in the middle of the school ladder.

The middle school rationale

As implied by the above reference to Johnson's 1962 treatment of the junior high school ("education's problem child," he called it), the clearest source of the emergent middle school lies in the almost insurmountable difficulties of the junior high school. Paul Woodring observed over three years ago that "it now appears that the 6-3-3 plan, with its junior high school, is on the way out." Sixty years' experience with the grade 7-9 junior high school has not succeeded in establishing the model junior high school pattern as appropriate schooling for children moving from childhood to adolescence. Despite such protestations as Samuel Popper's claim that "what over the years we have come to know as the junior high school is institutionally America's middle school," what is involved is far more than a label. However honorable its inception as a school to ease the transition from elementary to high school, the junior high school became a "junior" in fact to the high school. Despite many exceptions, especially in the grade 6-8 structures of suburban communities that never relinquished the four year high school, the grade 7-9 junior high school became the typical and now the traditional, soon-to-vanish (or be remodeled) school in the middle. But it was never really the middle, mathematically or programmatically, and tended to foist on children in the middle of their development from childhood to adolescence an organization and program copied directly from the school for full-blown adolescence, the high school.

Not all leaders of the new middle schools see their objective as that of seeking primarily to overcome the alleged failures of the junior high. My survey of middle schools last year (1967-68) included a checklist of reasons for the establishment of 110 middle schools in 10 percent random sample. This query yielded the following ranking of reasons (each respondent could check as many reasons as appropriate):

Reason	Schools Reporting
To eliminate crowded conditions in other schools -	64 — 58.2%
To provide a program specifically designed for students in this age group -	49 — 44.6%
To better bridge the elementary and the high school -	44 — 40.0%
To provide more specialization in grades five and/or six -	33 — 30.0%
To move grade nine into the high school -	27 — 24.5%

To remedy the weaknesses of the junior high school -	27 — 24.4%
To try out various innovations -	26 — 23.6%
To utilize a new school building -	23 — 20.9%
To use plans that have been successful in other school systems -	14 — 12.7%
To aid desegregation -	7 — 6.4%
Other -	13 — 11%

Several of these reasons other than "to remedy the weaknesses of the junior high school" do imply an inadequacy of the junior high school: "to provide a program specifically designed for students in this age group" (certainly it may be inferred that the junior high school has not done so); "to better bridge the elementary and the high school" (since the junior high school has not been the bridge it was intended to be?); and "to move grade nine into the high school" (again the question: Has the junior high school failed to provide for ninth-graders?).

But a full review of the rationale of the new school in the middle must recognize the inadequacies of the traditional elementary school model, too. One-third of the schools in this sample were said to have been established, in part, "to provide more specialization in grades five and/or six." Discontent with the self-contained classroom of the traditional elementary school has been rampant; yet many educators are unwilling to accept the all-too-easy and prevalent correction that merely substitutes the departmentalized pattern of the secondary school.

To me, however, the true rationale of the emergent middle school is rooted positively in the nature of the child and his development, rather than negatively in the inadequacies, even failures, of existing institutional arrangements. This rationale was stated elsewhere in these words I do not know how to put differently and better:

What, then, is the emergent middle school? To us, it is a school providing a program planned for a range of older children, preadolescents, and early adolescents that builds upon the elementary school program for earlier childhood and in turn is built upon by the high school's program for adolescence. Specifically, it focuses on the educational needs of what we have termed the "in-between-ager," although its clientele inevitably includes a few children for whom puberty may arrive before or after the middle school period. It is a school having a much less homogenous population, on the criterion of developmental level, than either the elementary or high school, with their concentration on childhood or adolescence.

Thus, the emergent middle school may be best thought of a phase and program of schooling bridging but differing from the childhood and adolescent phases and programs.

In short, the overriding reason for a new school in the middle, is to provide a program of schooling really suited to the needs of children in the middle, from childhood to adolescence. In providing such a program many related but basically subordinate reasons such as those cited herein are also to be considered.

The current movement

Various partial surveys and many observations of the past few years have cited the trend toward establishment of new schools in the middle.

My 1967-68 survey cited above was undertaken to provide more precise and comprehensive data regarding the nature and extent of this movement. This survey very clearly confirmed that there is indeed a nationwide movement toward new school organizations in the middle of the school ladder. Note these highlights of the findings:

1. A total of 1,101 schools in 37 of the 50 states were identified as middle schools (in the survey, "a school which combines into one organization and facility certain school years – usually grades 5-8 or 6-8 – which have in the past usually been separated in elementary and secondary schools under such plans as the 6-3-3, 6-2-4, and 6-6"). This number is more than twice that

identified by Cuff's 1965-66 survey, which yielded roughly comparable data as to the number of such schools.

2. Of the random sample (10 percent) of 110 middle schools studied more intensively, only 10.4 percent had been established before 1960, and 42.9 percent were established in 1966 and 1967.

3. Analysis of program and organizational arrangements of the schools in the sample showed that despite some interesting and promising exceptions, the middle schools in most cases (the number varying by each of many factors studied) were so far failing to provide a program and institutional organization differing very much from those in the predecessor schools, especially in the grade 7-9 junior high school. In fact, many so-called "new middle schools" appeared more like "junior, junior high schools."

4. More encouraging, many principals wrote in statements about plans underway to evaluate, replan, modify, or otherwise to break away more completely from the past. Also, even the current data revealed a marked increase in such promising and differing arrangements as extended exploration opportunities and other provisions for individualization; independent study plans, modular and other scheduling plans breaking sharply from conventional practice in both junior high and elementary school plans; and the emergence of team teaching, block-of-time combinations, small group-large group patterns which were essentially different from the model patterns of departmentalization and self-containment.

The movement continues to grow, very rapidly. During the year since my original list of middle schools was identified, reports received from several state departments of education as to increased numbers, a considerable volume of correspondence from school districts just this year (1968-69) moving into or planning new middle schools, and sundry other bits of information are convincing as to the burgeoning movement toward new schools in the middle. To me, the point of greatest concern is that the rapidity of the movement may once again freeze too hastily planned (or unplanned) institutional arrangements into what should be an ever-evolving and changing program of schooling to meet ever-changing needs of growing individuals in a dynamic society.

The middle school's opportunity

But the emergent middle school is just emerging. It is already late to halt its natural imitation of prior forms, but not too late. Some of the new forms are imaginative, rooted in the dreams of school people and laymen for a better education for the children of their communities. Traditional concepts of grade and group organization have been abandoned. Focus has been placed in these schools – admittedly all too few, but still the prototypes being recommended for testing and visitation – on the transescent child and his educational needs.

It is in these pioneer middle schools that new forms are being tested, sometimes undoubtedly with results discouraging to both the tester and the observers, but certainly in the spirit of experimentation critically needed in the improvement of American education. It is in this quest for better education that the new school in the middle finds its real opportunity and challenge. This advocate – if indeed I can be termed such – sees as a principal advantage of the new organization its potential for affecting the total school ladder and its program of education. Moving from the middle school, leaders can go both up and down, simultaneously, to effect major changes from normative school gradations to a fundamental focus on the developing individual. New prototypes of educational practice – tested, modified, and eventually used in the middle – can be re-adapted and again tried out in modified form in the lower and upper levels of schooling.

And of course, the real opportunity of the middle school is that of a testing ground for new and promising programs and practices that seem likely to be better for the transescent and perhaps to have a significant impact on the total program of public school education.

Some cautions and reservations

The most worrisome aspect of the current middle school movement is its bandwagon nature. Far too many middle schools have been created by administrative fiat to solve a population, building, or desegregation program – with little real planning of the program, organization, staff, and facility needed to provide adequate education and sound experimentation. In such situations the obvious thing is done: simply adopt lock, stock, and barrel the organization and program of the prior elementary and junior high school grades and transfer in the same personnel or merely leave them in the same building with no change other than in the grades and ages. It is little wonder that many educators are skeptical about the middle school movement!

These suggestions are offered to help districts moving toward new middle schools or seeking, even belatedly, to find better programs for schools recently changed from junior high to middle school status:

1. Build program and organizational, staffing, and building plans on the basis of careful, extended study of the nature of the transescent population by the staff concerned.

2. Defer visitation of other middle schools and program planning until Step No. 1 above has been taken, and build whatever plans are made from the ground up – working with the elementary school staffs concerned, evaluating existing programs rigorously, and inviting staff members, children and their parents, and any other interested persons to get their suggestions into the screening-planning process.

3. Wherever possible, introduce new programs and practices experimentally, with controls of some recognizable type to yield comparative data that will give more than guesses as to what works and what does not work.

4. Avoid like the plague too early publicity, visitation, external evaluation, and other dangers that will cause innovative teachers either to draw back to safety to escape unfavorable criticism or to go beyond the grounds of prudence to receive recognition.

5. Most important, budget for the extra costs of advance planning (including release of principal and some staff months in advance of the school's opening), and for experimentation

with evaluation (including the appointment of some person specifically qualified to lead in the experimentation process).

Conclusion – a prediction

As carefully as I have tried to observe and follow the middle school movement, I would not dare predict many details of what's ahead. One thing seems certain: For the foreseeable future middle schools of grades 5-8 or 6-8 are destined to replace the traditional grade 7-9 junior high schools as the schools in the middle. Whether the movement is simply another swing of the school ladder pendulum or a long overdue provision of better education at least for the middle-school-aged population remains to be seen. My guess is that the forces of educational change are so great and the emphasis on research and evaluation so impressive the new schools will increasingly be better planned and evaluated and therefore more effective. ▶

Reprinted with permission of *Phi Delta Kappan* (V. 50, #6, pp 355-7)

C. Kenneth McEwin reflects
for William Alexander...

Concepts of Continuing Importance

B eing invited to stand in Bill Alexander's stead and provide comments that I think Bill might have written is a distinct honor – and a daunting assignment. Identifying his many important professional accomplishments is not difficult, but deciding which of them to include here and how to adequately describe them is more challenging. Since the scope of his work, especially in the field of curriculum, spans such a broad range of areas in education, it seemed necessary to narrow the focus of these introductory statements to a particular aspect of his work. Considering the overall purposes of this historical publication, I have focused on his key role in the national reform movement to create a new educational institution designed to provide developmentally responsive schooling for young adolescents – the American middle school.

William Alexander did not singlehandedly create the middle school and certainly did not ever claim to have done so. When his pivotal role in this effort was mentioned, he always modestly pointed out the key contributions made by others, including those featured in this book. His pioneering efforts in the creation of and advocacy for this new institution, however, resulted in his being respectfully known as the "Father of the American Middle School." Bill was a man of real intellect, integrity, and insight who was greatly respected by his students and colleagues as well as those outside the education field.

My best judgments about what Bill would have written to follow the examples of his early writings included in this volume are based, in part, on the many conversations we had from the mid-1970s through the mid-1990s. I have also reread many of his published and unpublished works in the attempt to capture some of his strongest beliefs about middle school education. I was fortunate enough to know Bill as a colleague, friend, and mentor for many years. The lessons I learned from him about dedication to the education and welfare of our nation's youth remain with me and powerfully influence my professional decision making. It is my hope that those who did not have the opportunity to learn directly from Bill will now do so through exploring the rich legacy of knowledge he left us in his more than 200 professional publications which are merely sampled here.

William Alexander's influence extended far beyond middle level education. However, middle school education was clearly a favorite area. Several years ago, when I asked him what he considered to be his most significant work and what he had enjoyed most, he stated that his middle school work was closest to his heart and was most likely his most important professional contribution. It is fortunate for young adolescents, and those who serve them, that he selected the middle level as his greatest interest.

Bill was not only a man of thought, but also a man who took action on his beliefs. He challenged the powerful traditions associated with the junior high school and carefully laid out avenues to be taken to improve middle level education. As readers of these articles will quickly understand, the ideas he proposed in the 1960s remain as valid today as they were then.

Some of the seminal concepts which were part of the blueprint provided by William Alexander for the new middle school he proposed are provided below to help provide a frame of reference for those not familiar with his early work. Readers are urged to explore these concepts as well as his more recent work to enhance their understanding of the key aspects of effective middle level schooling as viewed by one of our most influential middle level educators. The order of these concepts is not intended to imply levels of priority.

- Middle schools should serve the unique developmental needs of young adolescents rather than being extensions of elementary schools or miniature models of senior high schools.

- The grade organization of middle schools is a significant factor for many reasons including the importance of grouping those who are most alike developmentally together in their own school where they can receive the full attention of all those who serve them.
- Effective middle schools should help ease the transition from elementary to high schools and from childhood to adolescence through many avenues including carefully laid out articulation efforts.
- Young adolescents should be taught by teachers who have received professional preparation that focused on the specialized knowledge, skills, and dispositions needed to enable them to be highly successful.
- All young adolescents should be assisted in obtaining optimum mastery of skills for continued learning.
- A major focus of middle schools should be on providing many opportunities for the healthy personal development of young adolescents.
- General education (organized knowledge) should be a strong focus of the middle school curriculum with every student acquiring a functional body of fundamental knowledge.
- The middle school curriculum should be flexible enough to allow young adolescents to progress at different rates and to different depths while providing abundant opportunities for exploration of interests.
- The middle school curriculum should include a strong emphasis on broad-based exploratory programs.
- The curriculum should be designed to provide continuity in total school programs and in each young adolescent's program.
- The middle school curriculum should provide opportunities for young adolescents to learn about values.
- All students in middle schools should be well-known as persons by at least one adult at school who accepts responsibility for their guidance.
- Middle schools should utilize an interdisciplinary organization with a flexibly scheduled day.

- Opportunities for learning how to develop decision-making and problem-solving skills should be provided for all middle school students.
- Varied and effective instructional strategies should be widely utilized.
- Tracking practices should be eliminated or greatly curtailed since ability grouping tends to hide the needs of individuals rather than meet them.
- Individualized instruction should be provided for all young adolescents.
- Middle school educators should work collaboratively with parents and other family members.
- Strong health and physical education programs should be a part of all middle schools.
- Middle school teachers should work in teams and have common planning periods.

Reviewing this rather comprehensive list may lead one to speculate on the extent to which these and related aspects of middle level schooling have been accomplished. When Bill was asked this question, he frequently responded with both encouragement about the many successes of the middle school movement and disappointment regarding the lack of authentic changes made at some of the newly reorganized schools. He clearly understood the complexity of a national reorganization of schooling but considered the glass "half-full" rather than "half-empty." He knew that young adolescents attending middle schools were much more likely to benefit from developmentally responsive programs than those attending traditional junior high schools or schools using other forms of grade organization. This acknowledgment, however, did not deter his career-long efforts to advocate for the universal implementation of middle schools that serve all young adolescents well.

When reflecting on Bill's satisfactions, concerns, and disappointments, I believe that one of the things in his professional life that he found most satisfying was the existence and growth of a national movement to create developmentally responsive middle schools. He was proud that he had been able to help draw attention to the need for this reform movement and hoped that his efforts had helped in some small way. He was also very pleased about the founding of National Middle School Association and believed that its existence significantly raised the possibility of widespread success for the middle school movement.

As would be expected, Bill's disappointments were closely related to his hopes. His greatest disappointment was that the changes that are required to provide young adolescents with the kind of schooling they so desperately need and deserve are not being made more quickly. An additional major concern he frequently expressed was the failure of teacher preparation institutions to implement specialized preservice and inservice programs which provide middle level teachers, administrators, and other professional personnel with the specialized knowledge, skills, and dispositions they need to be highly successful. He also believed that middle level educators have not worked hard enough at helping the general public understand the purposes and potential of middle level schools.

William M. Alexander was always a person with hope and confidence for the future. He focused on past failures only long enough to plan future actions that would improve circumstances. He respected his students, colleagues, and friends and cherished the opportunities he had to help advance worthy educational causes. Bill did not seek the spotlight for his many professional accomplishments and was interested in the middle school movement only because of its potential to enrich the lives of young adolescents.

I believe if Bill were writing this reflection piece, he would now turn the focus directly toward trying to get readers to understand the power they hold to help redirect middle school education in many of the positive directions in which it is now heading. He would also likely include a warning that without widespread support and concerted action on the part of all concerned, there is always the chance that the middle school movement will achieve only limited success. It would be his hope that everyone reading this book would make renewed commitments to helping middle level schools live up to their promise of helping all young adolescents reach their full potentials. ▶

II

Donald H. Eichhorn

*As was true with Dr. Alexander, most of my early elaborations on the middle school concept were oral presentations. Included here are two of these. The first was given in 1967 at a conference on "The Middle School Idea" held at the University of Toledo. The second was a presentation I made ten years later at an ASCD conference in Houston, Texas. Between them is a fairly long piece that was a chapter in an ASCD publication, **The School of the Future — Now** that was released in 1972. I believe that these pieces present a consistent philosophy, one I still hold to and believe to be valid.*

DONALD H. EICHHORN

New Knowledge
of 10- Through 13-Year-Olds

Paper presented at the Conference on "The Middle School Idea," November 11, 1967, at the College of Education, University of Toledo

E ducation in the latter half of the twentieth century faces serious challenges. Underlying these challenges are elements of a constant and accelerating change taking place in technology, in human growth and development, in sociological structures, and in expanding knowledge. While these developments have a profound effect on society in general, their impact on education is especially significant. Miller (1964) states this effectively:

> Dynamic forces are working with incredible speed today. Man is advancing so rapidly that new knowledge and technology confront him before he has fully understood past achievements. Keeping abreast of developments requires running fast just to keep up. Probably nowhere else does this rapid change present greater problems than in public education. Progress in knowledge itself, in instructional technology, and in school design greatly complicate the problems of education. The generation now in school will spend its adult years in a society that probably will be as radically different from today's as the society of the sixties is from that of the early twentieth century. (p. 7)

Previously accepted patterns of graded organizations, curricular programs, and teaching methodology appear unable to cope with the dynamic and complex societal needs of today.

Due to cultural factors physical maturation is occurring in individuals at an earlier chronological age than formerly; this trend is accompanied by similar trends in social interest. It is characteristic of American education to develop organizational patterns commensurate with the nature of its students; the current status of human growth and development suggests there is a definite need for re-examining the transitional school organization in light of changing physical and social traits of students.

A school organization emerging out of cultural change is not unique in American education. The philosophic base of the junior high school developed as a result of diverse pressures. In this regard, Lounsbury (1960) states:

> In some instances, even the champions of the junior high school movement came from different philosophic camps. College men advocated reorganization for economy of time. Public school leaders were concerned over better meeting immediate needs and saw the junior high school as a means of doing this. Board of education members may have seen reorganization as an economy move, while teachers may have supported reorganization because it would bring about new and improved special facilities such as science laboratories. (p. 147)

All of these concerns, administrative costs, elimination studies, and the concept of the differences found in adolescence, provided the spark which ignited the junior high school movement. Approximately sixty years later, the junior high school is an integral part of the American educational system, and it has firmly established the need for a transitional school between elementary school and high school. In this regard Grambs, Noyce, Patterson, and Robertson (1961) relate:

> That this innovation did satisfy many needs is evidenced by the phenomenal growth of the junior high in one form or another. The first junior high school opened in 1909. Today, only little better than half-century later, 82 per cent of the secondary school pupils are in districts which include some special kind of institutional arrangement to provide for the junior high school years. (p. 8)

Despite this favorable growth, there has been a persistent voice of criticism. Rice (1964) indicates:

> The pattern of the junior high school closely parallels the senior high school, but with so little evidence to justify it. It apes the senior high school in athletics, social events, class scheduling, and departmentalization. Its curriculum is pushed down from the grades above it, so that in all too many instances it really is a prep school for the senior high school. (p. 30)

The present structure of the junior high school philosophically moves in one direction while in actuality it operates contradictory to this philosophic base.

In this regard, Grambs, Noyce, Patterson, and Robertson (1961) intimate that the problem of the junior high school lies in the fact that it is essentially a coalition:

> Today's junior high school is essentially a hybrid. The seventh and eighth grades, while formerly restructured in the direction of secondary patterns, retain some of the flavor, character, and content of the elementary school. The ninth grade, brought into the junior high school from the senior high school is closely tied to the forms and traditions of the latter . . . .(p. 8)

To state that youngsters in the proposed middle school are either prepubescents, early adolescents, or adolescents cannot be justified. In reality, the transitional school includes boys and girls from all of these designations. Eichhorn (1966) suggests for clarification purposes the following definition:

> Transescence: the stage of development which begins prior to the onset of puberty and extends through the early stages of adolescence. Since puberty does not occur for all precisely at the same chronological age in human development, the transescent intellectual changes that appear prior to the puberty cycle to the time in which the

body gains a practical degree of stabilization over these complex pubescent changes. (p. 3)

The belief that transescence forms a compatible social grouping is the foundation for restructuring the transitional school organization. That a grouping of students with similar elements comprises a social system is described by Havinghurst and Neugarten (1957):

> The school may be viewed as a social system in much the same way as the family or peer group. Like the family or the peer group, the school acts as one of society's agents in socializing the child and in transmitting the culture. Also like the family or the peer group, the school has a subculture of its own - a complex set of beliefs, values and traditions, ways of thinking and behaving – that differentiate it from other social institutions. (p. 181)

It is essential to analyze the current changing status of the various idiographic forces as they apply to transescence. Presently, a marked trend in physical development is occurring. In this regard, Tanner (1963) reports:

> During the last 100 years there has been a very striking tendency for the time of adolescence, as typified by menarche or the growth spurt, to become earlier. The data on heights and weights of children of school age and before show that the whole process of growth has been progressively speeded up and that all age children born in the 1930s or 1950s for example were considerably larger than those born in the 1900s . . . The magnitude of the secular trend is very considerable and dwarfs the differences between socioeconomic classes and between geographical regions within countries such as Sweden and the United States. (pp. 143-144)

The trend in the United States is comparable to that reported throughout the Western World. Meredith (1941) cites that in an age group from nine to fourteen years that, "Boys living in the United

States, white and Negro, are 6 to 8 percent taller and 12 to 15 percent heavier than was the case half a century ago" (p. 932).

Mills (1950) suggests a similar development in relating that this growth tide has resulted in a four-inch increase in stature in America and a steady year-by-year increase in height and weight among freshmen matriculating in American colleges.

Espenschade and Meleney (1961), in a comparative study involving youngsters in the same school over a period from 1934-1935 to 1958-1959, found that girls in the later sample were one inch taller and six pounds heavier and that boys in the more recent study were over two inches taller and ten pounds heavier.

Commensurate with these reports of growth trends there exists a similar phenomenon in the earlier onset of menarche and sexual maturation. Tanner (1963) describes this acceleration in these words:

> The acceleration of growth is also shown in the marked secular trend in age of menarche . . . the average ages at menarche from 1830 to 1960 in Norway, Sweden, Finland, Great Britain, and Germany together with data from entrants to a woman's college in the United States . . . . The trend is remarkably similar in all the series, and over the whole period plotted. Age at menarche has been getting earlier by some 4 months per decade in Western Europe over the period 1830-1960. Other European data... and other American data, though not quite so regular, agree well with these figures. The trend in height and weight at about this age is closely equivalent to this amount of 4 months per decade, children of 10 thirty years ago having the size of children of 9 at present. (p. 143-144)

There is considerable research evidence indicating the basic causes of earlier maturation are directly linked to socioeconomic conditions. Generally, one postulates that the current trend toward earlier physical maturation, barring catastrophic events, will continue.

While impressive, earlier maturation would have little significance if it were not for the relationship between physical growth and social development. Stone and Barker (1939) in an earlier study reported that a greater proportion of postmenarchial girls than premenarchial girls of the same chronological age indicate a greater interest in personal adornment and day dreaming activities. Faust (1960) found that prestige was enhanced if menstruation had been experienced. In a similar vein, Jones and Bayley (1950) rated early maturing boys as more relaxed, more grown-up and more likely to have older friends.

In addition, there is evidence that interest patterns are emerging earlier in today's society. Jones (1960) in a study comparing attitudes and interests of three ninth grade classes in the same school but separated by 18 and 24 years (1935, 1953, 1959), found a greater maturity of heterosexual interests in the later classes than in 1935. Harris (1959) furthers this contention by stating, "Today youth marry younger and show an earlier interest in social relations . . . ." (p. 453-459)

While the major emphasis in transecence is on physical and social changes, mental growth also appears to be in a similar stage of transition. Inhelder and Piaget (1958) by means of intensive study of children have indicated that mental growth takes place according to well-defined stages. Children in the elementary school are considered in a stage known as concrete operations. Flavell (1963) effectively describes this stage in the following passage:

> . . . the starting point for concrete operations. . . is always the real rather than the potential. The child of 7-11 years acts as though his primary tasks were to organize and order what is immediately present; the limited extrapolation of this organizing and ordering to the 'not-there' is something he will do where necessary, but this extrapolation is seen as a special case activity. What he does not do (and what the adolescent does do) is delineate all possible eventualities at the outset...(p. 165)

The third and final stage of intellectual development, according to Piaget, is the formal operations stage. This level occurs after the attainment of concrete operations and usually comes into existence during the period of transecence. Again, a basic facet of development in transition. Bruner (1959) describes this stage as follows:

> After two decades of research, Piaget and his associates
> have traced the development of thinking to the stage
> where contemporary Western man reaches his full logical
> powers . . . Somewhere between 12 and 14 years of age,
> with the development of ability to reflect upon thought
> itself, the adolescent begins to show the marks of formal
> thinking. He is now ready to take his place as a scientist,
> a thinker, a spinner of theory. (p. 363)

Similar to earlier physical maturation, there appears to be an acceleration of mental maturation. Our society provides considerable cognitive experiences in an ever-increasing manner. The effect of experience plays an important role with regard to the onset of formal operations in the Piagetian theory. Inhelder and Piaget (1958) comment on this role in this way:

> . . . the age of 11-12 years may be, beyond neurological
> factors, a product of progressive acceleration of individual
> development under the influence of educations, and
> perhaps nothing stands in the way of further reduction of
> the average age in a more or less distant future . . . . A
> particular social environment remains indispensable for
> the realization of these possibilities. It follows that their
> realization can be accelerated or retarded as a function of
> cultural and educational conditions. (p. 337)

It appears that undoubtedly, educational and cultural experiences will continue to expand for every group in our society. For example, programs such as "headstart" are well underway.

A third significant dimension of transescence concerns the youngster's evolving social status in which the transescent shifts from a dependence on parents and home for personal security, interests and values to reliance on the peer group.

The process by which a youngster moves from a dependent to an independent status in our society is a process of emancipation and is related to our culture. Parsons (1963) states in this regard:

> It is at this point of emergence into adolescence that a set of patterns and behavior phenomena which involves a highly complex combination of age grading and sex role elements begins to develop. These may be referred to together as the phenomena of the "youth culture." Certain of its elements are present in preadolescence and others in adult culture. But the peculiar combination in connection with this particular age level is unique and highly distinctive of American society. (p. 160)

The transfer of the security base from the family to the peer group appears to begin early in transescence and reaches its zenith in adolescence. Gesell, Ilg, and Ames (1956) point out in this regard:

> If ever the word family acquires its true meaning, it is when the child is ten years of age. Ten not only accepts but likes his lot. In fact no other father or mother seems to surpass his in his own eyes . . . This is the last age for some time to come when the child enters into a family excursion with casual thoughtfulness, adaptability, and full enjoyment. (p. 54)

Contrast this description with Coleman's (1961) analysis of the adolescent:

> With his fellows, he comes to constitute a small society, one that has most of its important interaction within itself, and maintains only a few threads of connection with the outside adult society. In our modern world of mass communication and rapid diffusion of ideas and knowledge, it is hard to realize that subcultures can exist right under the very noses of adult subcultures with languages

all their own, with special symbols, and most importantly, with value systems that may differ from adults. (p. 3)

Thus, transescence also is an age of transition from dependence to independence with regard to the security base of the family.

Major emphasis in this paper has been placed on the changing nature of the 10- to 13-year-old. It has been suggested that the biological development of youth in the past century has undergone a significant trend toward earlier physical and mental maturation in relation to chronological age. This phenomenon, due largely to highly favorable socioeconomic factors, shows little indication of abating. Culturally, a comparable trend is evident and expresses itself in the earlier emergence of interests and attitudes previously attributed to later life. Since this pattern also is imbedded in a favorable cultural era, it appears likely that this trend will also continue as opportunities for enriched experiences rapidly accelerate and occasions for broader peer involvement through technological developments increase.

As democracy's medium for the transmission of cultural values, education must alter basic patterns if it is to accomplish effectively its inherent role. Alterations should be predicated on the nature of the learner as well as the expectations of society. In one respect, the educator must recognize that the transescent child is maturing at an earlier age and in doing so creates personal needs which challenge personal security. In the same vein, the educator has to consider the impact of a significantly changing culture on youth. It is imperative that transecents learn to interact with a constantly changing way of life through the development of life processes suited to the understanding, adjustment, and control of all aspects of rapid change.

The middle school concept, founded in the dramatic developments in human growth and development as well as in the society in which youngsters interact, may emerge into a successful organizational pattern, but only if educators develop programs commensurate with the characteristics of the 10 to 13 year old in all respects. ▶

References

Bruner, J.S. (1959). Inhelder and Piaget's the growth of logical thinking: A psychologists' viewpoint. *British Journal of Psychology, L,* 363.

Coleman, J.S. (1961). *The adolescent society.* New York: Cromwell-Collier Publishing Co.

Eichhorn, D.H. (1966). *The middle school.* New York: The Center for Applied Research ln Education, Inc.

Espenschade, A., & Meleney, H. (1961). Motor performance of boys and girls. *The Research Quarterly of the American Association of Health, Physical Education and Recreation, XXXII,* 187.

Faust, M. (1960). Developmental maturity as a detriment in prestige of adolescent girls. *Child Development, XXXI,* 182-183.

Flavell, J. (1963). *The developmental psychology of Jean Piaget.* New York: D. Van Nostrand Company, Inc.

Gesell, A., Ilg, F., & Ames, L. (1956). *Youth, the years from ten to sixteen.* New York: Harper and Row.

Grambs, J.D., Noyce, C.G., Patterson, F., & Robertson, J. (1961). *The junior high school we need.* Alexandria, VA: The Association of Supervision and Curriculum Development.

Harris, D.B. (1959). Sex differences in the life problems and interests of adolescents, 1935 and 1957. *Child Development XYX,* 453-459

Havighurst, R.J., & Neugarten, B. (1957). *Society and education.* Boston: Allyn and Bacon, Inc.

Inhelder, B., & Piaget, J. (1958). *The growth of logical thinking from childhood to adolescence.* New York: Basic Books, Inc.

Jones, M.C. (1960). A comparison of the attitudes and interests of ninth grade students over two decades. *Journal of Educational Psychology, LI,* 175-186.

Jones, M.C., & Bayley, N. (1950). Physical maturing among boys as related to behavior. *Journal of Educational Psychology, XLI,* 129-148.

Lounsbury, J.H. (1960). How the junior high school came to be. *Educational Leadership, XVIII,* 147.

Meredith, H.V. (1941). Stature and weight of children of the United States with reference to the influence of racial, regional, socio-economic and secular factors. *American Journal of Diseases of Childhood, LXII,* 932.

Miller, R.I. (1964). *Education in a changing society*, Washington, DC: National Education Association, Project on the Instructional Program.

Mills, C.A. (1950). Temperature influence over human growth and development. *Human Biology, XXII*, 71.

Parsons, T. (1963). Age and sex in the social structure of the United States. In Warren Kallenbach and Harold M. Hodges (Eds.), *Education and society*. Columbus: OH: Charles E. Merrill Books, Inc.

Rice, A.H. (1964). What is wrong with junior highs? Nearly everything. *Nations Schools, 74,* 30.

Stone, C.P., & Barker, R.G. (1939). The attitudes and interests of premenarcheal and postmenarcheal girls. *Journal of Genetic Psychology, LIV,* 61-62.

Tanner, J.M. (1963). *Growth at adolescence*. Oxford: Blackwell Scientific Publications.

The Emerging
Adolescent School of the Future — Now

Published in *The School of the Future – Now*, J. Galen Saylor (Ed.),
ASCD, 1972

A point of departure in an analysis of school program is, the writer believes, the broad, general goals upon which program develops. While there is little precise agreement regarding the nature and function of a specific program for the middle school level, there is to some degree a general consensus on broad goals. It is helpful to highlight briefly a few of these goals.

Goals of Emerging Adolescent Education

First, the emerging adolescent school should contribute to the development of values. Students in the years 10 to 14 are at a stage in which value orientation is undergoing a transition from a family, adult base to a peer orientation. Youngsters are searching for deeper understandings of relations with peers, family, adults, and society. The school has a rich opportunity to provide activities which will enhance growth in value patterns. Schools will vary in specific approach, but it seems essential that a basic role of the school is to assist students in acquiring values.

In this respect, the climate of the school is indeed vital. The tendency has been to equate learning with fear, repression, and joylessness. The values inherent in such an approach are suspect in areas relating to an individual's mental health as well as those relating to society in general.

Unquestionably, learning can take place in a restrictive environment. On occasion, authors have argued for the values inherent in such an approach. Hudson comments:

My own suspicion is that progressive schools do make most children happier than authoritarian ones; but that they withdraw from children the cutting edge that insecurity, competition, and resentment supply. If we adjust children to themselves and each other, we may remove from them the springs of their intellectual and artistic productivity. (p. 134)

This point of view has been periodically accepted by U.S. educators. Certainly, the return to rigid subject-centered curricula of the sixties is a case in point. The question emerges as to what values are most appropriate to the cultural goals of the seventies. Bruner (1971), after a decade of curricular experience, comments on this issue:

It [education] is a deeply political issue in which we guarantee a future for someone; and, frequently, in guaranteeing a future for someone, we deal somebody else out. If I had my choice now, in terms of a curriculum project for the seventies, it would be to find a means whereby we could bring society back to its sense of values and priorities in life. I believe I would be quite satisfied to declare, if not a moratorium, then something of a de-emphasis on matters that have to do with the structure of history, the structure of physics, the nature of mathematical consistency, and deal with curriculum rather in the context of the problems that face us. We might better concern ourselves with how those problems can be solved, not just by practical action, but by putting knowledge, wherever we find it and in whatever form we find it, to work in these massive tasks. (pp. 29-30)

Regarding these two divergent points of view, it seems that educators must view their validity in light of the nature of the emerging adolescent learner. The need of the emerging adolescent for intellectual curiosity, self-motivation, and intense peer interaction would seem to obtain more readily in a less rather than more rigid environment. This is not to say, however, that structure is unnecessary. The nature of the youngster at this level requires a security base and, as values emerge, a realistic degree of structure seems advisable.

Learning goal

A second goal for the school for the emerging adolescent involves the learning program. This is a crucial age for budding scholars. With the rapidity and diverseness of maturation, emerging adolescents are vulnerable as students. At this level, promising students have sometimes encountered learning problems far removed from mental ability. Conversely, student characteristics such as determination, enthusiasm, and curiosity provide unlimited potential for learning. By its philosophy of how learning takes place, a school can facilitate or retard student growth.

A number of aspects of the instructional program should be considered. The following list is indicative but not exhaustive:

1. *Individual Attention.* As students leave elementary school, the range of learning rates and competencies magnifies. It is essential to develop a curriculum and techniques which ensure maximum attention to the learning patterns within the dynamics of the individual learner. This does not imply that individualized attention should be equated only with a self-study approach. The emphasis should be placed on monitoring student performance, and measures should be taken to ensure maximum opportunity for development in either an individual or a group context. Early adolescents are at a stage in their development in which they need opportunities to assume responsibility which will lead to self-direction. Inherent in this approach is acceptance of consequences of choice as youngsters begin to see the relationship between choice and responsibility.

2. *Performance Basis.* Students should be expected to achieve to a realistic performance standard. This standard should be established, however, not as a group standard but as a personal standard. Through this approach, students hopefully will gain a critical understanding of their abilities and realize a sense of achievement

in relation to these competencies. This line of reasoning suggests that every student be expected to achieve learning mastery in relation to his personal standard.

3. *Learning Skills and Processes Versus Acquisition of Content.* Cognitively, the young adolescent is in transition between the concrete operations level of the elementary school and the formal operations stage of the high school. It is vital that emphasis be placed on higher cognitive processes such as hypothesizing, generalizing, synthesizing, and evaluating, as well as on the lower processes such as recalling, recognizing, repeating, and copying. Application of this emphasis again mandates consideration of the individual.

The argument that content is unimportant is not valid. Youngsters should gain considerable content knowledge. This acquisition, however, will not mean a set body of knowledge acquired by all students, but rather a wide range of content knowledge gained as an outgrowth of effort in skills and processes. For example, one student may achieve content knowledge related to the religions in Japan while another may learn a great deal about Japan's government. In both cases, however, the students will have acquired skills in gathering, analyzing, and evaluating data.

4. *Social or Interaction Skills and Processes.* In effect, social or interaction skills are necessary to function effectively in group situations. Group interaction is essential at this age. Such processes as identification, discrimination, clarification, challenge, debate, and compromise are skills in which young adolescents need competency. While these processes are closely related to the learning skills of self-study, they are employed in a different context in group interaction.

Similar to the previously expressed thought regarding content, considerable content learning may take place through the acquisition of social skills. This is a natural forum for analyzing problems relating to growth and development or the humanities. For example, science has provided our society with a highly cherished technology. A natural problem for group interaction would be to analyze the positive aspects of this technology while debating solutions to its negative aspects such as air pollution.

Personal development goal

A third goal of early adolescent education revolves around personal development. Possibly no aspect of emerging adolescent education is given more philosophic support than personal development. It is usually cited as a part of the rationale supporting the program. Research has clearly demonstrated the validity and necessity for inclusion of personal development in an educational program for this age. Wattenberg's (1969) perceptive analysis is characteristic. He writes:

> As we consider the many issues involved in creating
> middle schools, we must base what we do on a theory as
> to human development in the first half of the second
> decade of life and what are the forces which most affect
> that development. (p. 164)

In actual practice, unfortunately, few schools for early adolescents give more than superficial treatment to this goal despite exhortations to the contrary. To be effective, personal development instruction must be an integral part of the early adolescent's daily program.

Maturity, or the lack of it, is an important concern for emerging adolescents. This concern reflects itself in all aspects of a youngster's school life and influences his intellectual, social, and emotional progress. Bayley (1955), commenting on intellectual growth, states:

> It becomes evident that the intellectual growth of any
> child is a resultant of varied and complex factors. These
> will include his inherent capacities for growth, both in
> amount and in rate of progress. They will include the
> emotional climate in which he grows; whether he is
> encouraged or discouraged, whether his drive (or ego

involvement) is strong in intellectual thought processes or is directed to other aspects of his life field. And they will include the material environment in which he grows; the opportunities for experience and for learning and the extent to which these opportunities are continuously geared to his capacity to respond and to make use of them. Evidently all of these things are influential in varying amounts for different individuals and for different stages in their growth. (pp. 813-814)

Emotional development is crucial at this stage. As students move away from dependence on the family, social relationships become increasingly more vital in their lives. Thus, there is a need to develop a well-defined program in the area of peer relations. This program should have at least two dimensions. First, learning activities should be arranged to ensure maximum interaction with peers and adults. For example, a well-conceived student activity program is needed as part of the curriculum. The concept of "extracurricular" implies that these activity areas are external to program. The opposite approach is needed.

Second, there is need to include guidance programs which enable students to study, analyze, question, and discuss their personal growth and development with regard to relationships with family, friends, and adults. The typical health program falls far short of meeting this need. In most cases, this instruction is best achieved through informal discussions with trusted adults and peers. Emerging adolescents need the reassurance which comes from understanding the growth process. This understanding assists students in meeting the challenges of learning.

These few goals which have been related are not all-encompassing, but hopefully they will set the tone for subsequent program statements.

To suggest a singular pattern for emerging adolescent education of the future is complex at best. The diverse needs of inner city, suburban, and rural youth do not lend themselves well to pat solutions.

In addition, there are other limiting factors encountered in the reality of local situations such as the status of architectural design, budgets, teacher education, and professional expertise. Nevertheless, there has emerged, in the writer's judgment, sufficient professional awareness to make an attempt to suggest a fundamental pattern. Granted, organizational form will vary considerably from school to school; but organization is viewed here as a means to an end, not an end in itself.

Educational Program for Emerging Adolescent Learners

Curriculum

Three interrelated aspects of the instructional program will be analyzed: curriculum, strategy for learning, and grouping. Each will be treated in an eclectic manner.

The curriculum of the emerging adolescent school appears to have three dimensions. These are represented in Figure 1.

Figure 1 suggests basic principles for the emerging adolescent school program. These principles may be stated as follows:

The characteristics and needs of the emerging adolescent learner are central to school program development.

There are three fundamental curriculum needs. These include the acquisition of learning processes necessary for self education; the acrualization through self-awareness, understanding, and interaction; and the active involvement of the learner with knowledge as it relates to the various aspects of man's heritage and contribution.

1. *Learning Processes.* Fundamental to learning is the ability to acquire knowledge. This ability is a result of one's management of learning competencies. Skills and processes, thus, are essential to a self-directed learner. The school for emerging adolescents will be a laboratory in which every youngster will develop the mental skill processes necessary for advanced learning.

In the learning laboratory, each student will be involved in a self-pacing design which will facilitate acquisition of learning skills and processes. This design will vary from individual to individual according to the learner's current level of readiness and competency.

Figure 1.
Emerging Adolescent Curriculum

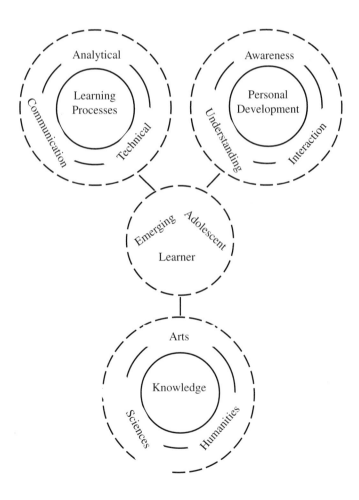

Emerging adolescents, irrespective of age or grade in school, possess a diverse range of abilities related to learning skills. This range extends from the concrete stage to the abstract; in addition, there are learning constraints such as auditory and visual perception problems which must be considered. Thus, the requirement that each emerging adolescent needs a highly specialized pattern becomes quite significant.

While there is a need to categorize skills and processes, this grouping should be a radical departure from the highly fragmented skill programs currently in effect. Rather, categorization should be on the nature of the skill, for example, communication, analytic, technical skills, and should stress similarities among them. Communication skills involve symbols and their visual and oral use. Analytical skills involve the practical application of skills and processes in logical thought such as gathering, analyzing, synthesizing, and evaluating data. There is an interrelationship between these broad categories which aids and reinforces. For example, boys and girls acquire information through reading and listening, and then communicate information orally or in writing after managing this information through higher cognitive processes. If emphasis is placed merely on acquisition of skills and processes, a vital link with cognitive growth is missed.

Technical skills are essential in areas such as industrial education, art, music, homemaking, and typing. These areas of development should play an important role during the emerging adolescent years and should be taught in a manner similar to the other skill areas of this component.

Apparently there are four general areas for skill and process learning. These include language, mathematics, science, and the practical and fine arts. While interrelated – and these interrelationships should be exploited – skills and processes within each generalized area should be given special attention. It should be emphasized that these general areas should not be equated with traditional content subjects, but rather should be treated as basic areas of logic, structure, symbolism, and process.

Student grouping in this component is by its nature highly individualistic. Architecture which permits an open, informal laboratory setting is most desirable. In this setting, students can work as individuals within larger informal areas. This facilitates the differentiation of materials, human resources, and independent programs necessary for self-study. Yet self-study can proceed in the context of a variety of learning programs. The size of the group can range from one to "X" number of students, depending upon the learning objectives involved. Informal groupings occur based upon social interests in conjunction with learning programs. This permits individual self-study as well as interaction to sharpen each youngster's progress. It also provides for peer compatibility as students can arrange themselves based on maturity and interests. Forced grouping based on group objectives seems to be neither effective nor desirable.

The teacher's role is to analyze learning patterns, construct learning programs for each student, and carefully monitor progress in relation to individual programs. Teachers must be intimately aware of current achievement and learning problems encountered with each student. They also must have expertise in a variety of teaching techniques, including independent, small, and large group approaches. It is particularly crucial that they be able to diagnose learning problems and suggest solutions.

2. *Knowledge Dimension.* Acquisition of knowledge is a vital aspect of the emerging adolescent's learning program. Although there is little attempt at promoting a set body of content knowledge, students will be heavily involved in a wide range of content learning. Man's past accomplishments, present challenges, and future aspirations will be the basis of this curriculum.

These elements will be taught in an integrated or interdisciplinary curriculum. Subject matter from the humanities, arts, and sciences will form the basis of this integration. This approach will have a thematic base out of which a whole range of interrelated topics will emerge.

This approach will emphasize content, but in a much different context. Youngsters will work with content in perspective. For example, a unit might involve technology and its relationship with science and government. In this approach, some students will study the historical evolution of technology and its many contributions as a result of scientific effort, while others will form governmental and community action groups to debate the issues and suggest solutions for problems encountered with technology's effect on the environment.

This phase of the curriculum should stress students' interests and capitalize on characteristics such as creativity and enthusiasm. There should be a strong emphasis on analyzing man's contributions, but also an equally strong emphasis on active involvement in man's relationships and problems within our culture.

Related areas such as art, music, and creative expression should be a part of this integrated curriculum. These areas are part of our culture and should be studied in context. There are, of course, skills and processes involved in these areas which certainly can be taught in the learning laboratory component; however, their cultural impact on man necessitates their inclusion in the knowledge phase of the curriculum.

The learning strategy which seems best to meet the reasoning of this component is one of individual inquiry and group interaction. Performance objectives should be designed around the social and interaction skills and processes basic to group involvement. Youngsters should actively pursue knowledge and be given the opportunity to seek creative solutions to issues and problems involved.

Student grouping in the component should be based on social maturity. Again, if these groupings are informally achieved simply through student choice, learning will be greatly enhanced. This grouping pattern should not be based on age or grade level, but rather on maturity.

Special interest activity programs which have used this approach, that is, activity selection based on interest regardless of grade, have met with considerable success.

The teacher's role in this component centers on the nature of the goals for instruction. Thus, a teacher will be asked to assist in the development of integrated themes, possess and use teaching skills which will facilitate student inquiry, and employ principles of group dynamics in the many interaction activities. In addition, a teacher must create an environment which promotes dynamic learning.

3. *Personal Development.* Personal development naturally is very much a part of the first two components discussed. Its vital importance, however, necessitates special emphasis.

Of significant importance for emerging adolescents is an understanding of physical growth. With an understanding of maturation, the youngster is able to cope with a very rapidly changing life pattern. Without such an awareness, a favorable self-concept will not occur and learning will be jeopardized. Some knowledge of physical-social growth is essential, but probably more important are opportunities for emerging adolescents to discuss peer and family relations. Unless the developing adolescent is aided in coping with the realities involved, particularly with current and persistent problems in relations with others, serious consequences often occur.

Instruction

Instruction may take many forms, ranging from group discussions to individual counseling. While the guidance staff plays an important role, the individual teacher, custodian, teacher aide, and secretary are the front line adults who must assume prime responsibility. Adults working with emerging adolescents should be well grounded in knowledge of age characteristics and possess techniques which permit them to function effectively with this maturation level. Sweeney (1971) summarizes this role by stating:

> The effective adult will be a person who sincerely values
> and cares about other people. He will be a good listener,
> i.e., a person who can understand both the verbal and
> nonverbal communication of the other person. In addition
> to being a good listener, he is able to communicate that

he has understood. This person could be described as
open to new or different ideas while still possessing a
philosophy of life that guides his behavior without
imposing it on others. He is a trusting person, one who is
aware that others may not be trustworthy at times, but
who is willing to be mistaken until proven otherwise. He
has a capacity for helping other persons to honestly
confront matters of relevance to them which are otherwise
too threatening or anxiety producing for them to cope
with rationally.

A number of programs could be suggested for personal development; but if a teaching staff reflects Sweeney's philosophy, almost
any program will enable youngsters to develop in the right perspective. One area of considerable importance, however, is the need for
an organization which requires that each youngster have direct
access to an adult who is intimately aware of this youngster in all
aspects of his life. This relationship must be based upon mutual
trust and respect so that the youngster feels secure and can function
responsibly.

In this section, an educational program has been suggested based
upon this writer's belief that any program for this age group must
be founded upon the age characteristics and educational needs of
youngster at this level.

Current Challenges in Emerging Adolescent Education

• *Can middle school educators move beyond the argument of
which grades should be in the middle/junior high school?*

This argument is grounded more in emotion than professional
logic. Assuming there is a separate level of maturation between the
childhood years of the elementary school and the adolescent years
of the high school, one must argue that a youngster, regardless of
years in school, should be placed at his level of maturation. This
precludes rigid differentiation between fifth and sixth grades and

between eighth and ninth grades. Anyone who has ever worked with emerging adolescent youngsters will attest to the fact that there are middle schoolers who belong in the high school and high schoolers who belong in the middle school.

If one attempts to analyze a "seventh grader," he might quickly discover that this youngster may be physically an adolescent, working at a sixth grade level in reading but achieving mathematics at an eighth grade level. The great diversity among middle school students suggests that for all practical purposes a graded structure is obsolete. Likewise to argue that the sixth grader belongs in the elementary school because the elementary principal feels that the sixth grade provides leadership is ill-advised and inconsequential. Rather the youngster and his need ought to be the focal point for placement.

This raises the issue of criteria for middle school placement. Should youngsters be grouped according to academic achievement, chronological age, physical and social maturity, or a combination of factors? At present we group youngsters based largely upon chronological age and academic achievement, with little reference to physical and social gradation. Is this defensible in light of the stated purposes of education for the emerging adolescent learner? Are we not in reality saying by our graded placement that the middle school is for the sixth, seventh, and eighth grade achiever – not for the early adolescent?

If the middle school is ultimately to reach its potential, the fundamental pupil arrangements for instruction must be based on physical-social maturity. Within this physical-social grouping, instruction should be structured in a continuous progress format so that students could progress as their abilities and interests permit. As has been suggested earlier, student grouping should be as informal as possible, that is, association by maturity level and interests rather than by forced grouping arrangements.

• *Can middle school educators develop proper perspective regarding the place and function of organizational technique?*

Educators of emerging adolescents traditionally have started with form and organization as an end rather than a means to an end. Theorists have expounded on ungradedness, departmentalization, core, team teaching, and modular scheduling as ways to ensure improvement in instruction.

There is no quarrel with any of these approaches because each has and can provide sound direction, given the right set of variables. What this writer quarrels with, however, is the attitude which implies that unless one fully subscribes to one or the other, the chance for instructional success is greatly reduced. Each school district's "chemistry" is different and what succeeds in one area is not necessarily going to succeed in another.

These devices should be considered as tools. For example, a top professional teacher will develop a learning objective and then select a technique which seems most applicable to success given a particular class, the state of available hardware and software, and appropriate time. His selection may range from class demonstration to a field trip. The typical administrator in the early adolescent school, conversely, will often apply an organizational approach regardless of staff interest and competence, in-service capability, or plant facility.

Administrative structure provides potential. It does not necessarily provide improved education. It behooves middle school educators to analyze carefully student characteristics and staff competencies, coming to any conclusions regarding organizational structure.

• *Can educators devise an acceptable method of reporting student progress?*

The traditional marking system has been devastating in its effect on attempts at improving education. Instructional processes which seem best for this age level center on the individual, while traditional systems are based upon group performance. By attempting to placate parents' demand for traditional marking, instructional improvement is either compromised or altered in such a manner that emphasis is returned to group techniques which facilitate group marking. This cycle either limits or defeats progress. The challenge is to develop a communications program so that parents are informed of a child's progress in a manner which is acceptable to the parents but which does not destroy program.

• *Can educators of emerging adolescents create an alliance with higher education, state departments of education, and professional associations?*

The principle of early adolescent education has been with us for more than a half century. The impact which it has had on higher education and state departments of education, with a few notable exceptions, has been remarkably limited. As one scans higher education offerings, one is dismayed by the paucity of training available to future middle school teachers. The prevailing attitude continues to be: prepare teachers for the elementary and high school and the middle/junior high school staffing will take care of itself.

The chief criticism is that this lack of emphasis deprives students, at a crucial period, of the professional expertise that the elementary school, and university levels enjoy. One cannot dispute the need for specialized teachers on the elementary and high school levels, but one finds it difficult to accept the position that middle or junior high teachers need less specialized training.

The basic problem is a lack of recognition that this level has traditionally received. State departments of education recognize elementary and secondary levels, assuming that the solution to problems such as certification and reimbursement can be applied to the school in the middle. The answer quite likely is not in creating further bureau structures, but in redesigning those in existence so that the attention necessary for this level to succeed will be forthcoming.

There is a crucial need for professional associations, representing all levels of education, to pool their talents in an effort to aid and support the development of program for youngsters in the middle. Elementary, secondary, and university leaders need to join the efforts of leaders in emerging adolescent education to find viable solutions. While school districts throughout this nation initiate changes in early adolescent education, progress is curtailed and even ended by restraints imposed by related agencies.

• *Will the middle school accept in practice the theory of uniqueness?*

Throughout the 20th century educators of early adolescents have proclaimed philosophically that they represent schools which bridge the elementary and high school levels. In practice this philosophy has meant that a student enters as of grade 6 or 7 a modified high school or, if you please, a modified adolescent school. Curricular programs all too often are adolescent programs – one step lower. Today, there are some indications that educators are beginning to view middle schools as extensions of the elementary or as schools for children – one step higher.

This writer is firmly convinced that research and logic have clearly indicated that there is a developmental level between the childhood years of the elementary school and the adolescent years of the high school. In the final analysis, there is only one middle school differentiation. This differentiation is the developmental uniqueness of its student clientele. On occasion, educators have stated that if all students could be placed into one building, there would be little necessity for organizational levels. This belief must be challenged on the grounds that there are different levels of physical, mental, and social development, and it is absurd to believe that schools can educate students in a physical-social vacuum.

Future

The future of any endeavor depends upon the expertise and commitment of its advocates. The emerging adolescent movement is no exception. There are many positive indications that educators of early adolescents in America today possess both of these ingredients in ample measure.

As has been indicated, there are significant challenges for successful implementation of the basic philosophy and program for schools in the middle. Possibly the greatest challenge for the future of middle school is the willingness of those committed to this organization to pioneer creative programs designed specifically for the early adolescent learner.

While in many cases these programs have yet to emerge, the future worth of this level of schooling demands that they be created.

The promise of middle level education lies in its potential. It presents educators with immense possibilities. If educators are content merely to apply the inadequate approaches of the past, middle schools will simply go the route of former organizations. If, however, educators are prepared to study the characteristics and needs of these unique students and initiate an imaginative approach to program development, the promise of the future for middle school education can be fulfilled. ▶

References

Bayley, N. (1955). On the growth of intelligence. *American Psychologist 10*, 813-814.

Bruner, J.S. (1971). The process of education reconsidered. In Robert R. Leeper (Ed.), *Dare to care/Dare to act* (pp. 29-30). Washington, DC: Association for Supervision and Curriculum Development.

Eckenrod, J.S., Hurd, P.D., Rasmussen, F., & Robinson, J. (1971). *Biological sciences curriculum study 'A multidisciplinary human sciences program for middle schools.'* Boulder, CO. Sponsored by the National Science Foundation.

Hudson, L. (1966). *Contrary imaginations: A psychological study of the English schoolboy.* London: Methuen & Co., Ltd.

Sweeney, T.J. (1971). *Adult models for the emerging adolescent.* Paper prepared for the meeting of the ASCD Council on the Emerging Adolescent Learner, Washington, DC.

Wattenberg, W. (1969). The middle school as one psychologist sees it. *High School Journal, 53* (3), 164.

Middle School: An Evolving Idea

Assembly address presented at the National ASCD Conference in Houston, Texas, March 21, 1977

This evening, I wish to concentrate my brief remarks on a remarkable idea. It is an idea that simply will not be overpowered. It is an idea which has provided educators with the opportunity to serve youngsters in the age span in a special way. It is an idea which has survived the constant philosophic battle between humanists and behaviorists. It is an idea which has ineptness and ignorance. It is an idea which has remained dynamic even when school programs, well intentioned but ill-conceived, have threatened its existence. It is an idea that began 70 years ago in this nation and is as beautiful an idea as it was in 1910. It is an idea which is often jilted but never wilts. It is which some have called the junior high and others have called the middle school.

I realize that in this audience this evening are women and men who have devoted their professional lives to this idea and who have worked tirelessly to make the dream of the middle school idea a reality.

The growth of middle schools during the past two decades has been remarkable. Not only the fact that the numbers of schools have grown by leaps and bounds, but one must also recognize the fact that these schools have grown in quality. It is inspiring to see the enormous growth in pride of young men and women who by their daily teaching activities have, for the first time in the history movement, given the idea status. It is an idea which has caught the enthusiasm of almost everyone it has touched. Serving the poor and the rich in cities and suburbs, the idea is slowly ascending to its rightful place in American education. Once referred to as the stepchild of American education, it now has become education's emerging adolescent full of promise and potential.

While we look to the future with considerable anticipation we should not forget the past. For in its past, there are clues for its future. If we are wise enough to consider those aspects of the junior high and middle schools which have led to barriers of progress, we will be able to ensure that this emerging adolescent of today becomes the adult of American education of tomorrow.

In my judgment, the major fundamental dilemma of the middle school lies in the bridge between theory and practice.

On one hand, we have consistently accepted the premise of uniqueness. On the other hand, in practice, we have accepted models of education which reject uniqueness. Constantly, leaders of the middle school movement are confronted with the question – What is different about middle schools? Why should the program differ?

Recently, I was conducting an in-service meeting in a very small rural coal town in Pennsylvania. One of the teachers who was very opposed to middle schools stated: "Since there is no difference between middle school students and high school students, why try to change?"

I reacted very badly and replied, "Why, of course there are differences and these are evident." However, I believe the position taken by this veteran teacher is the crux of the middle school dilemma. It was one of those occasions, however, in which two people gave totally different answers to the same question and both were right.

In support of his position, this teacher could point to the fact that students in 7th grade were studying what students in 10th grade were studying. Students were expected in 7th grade to learn in the manner of 10th grade students. Oh, sure, some 7th graders need more help in note-taking than most 10th graders, but the process is the same. The important aspect of the chapter on Japan in 10th grade deals with the same important aspects of the 7th grade book – so again these students are the same.

I countered these remarks by stating that the physical and social characteristics of the middle schooler are different and vary greatly from one student to another. The teacher agreed to this line of reasoning but countered with, "But what does have to do with it?"

It occurred to me the reason why we are still trying to develop middle school lies in that scenario. When Havighurst said, "The period from twelve to eighteen is primarily one of physical and social maturing...The principal lessons are emotional and social, not intellectual." We shouted, "Of course."

When Vars said, "Each individual grows according to his own timetable which varies from month to month and is not the same for all aspects of his development...a compounding of rapid change and highly variable growth patterns gives the middle school the most diverse student body of any school unit." we said, "Right, right – absolutely right."

When Strang said, "Bodily changes, especially if sudden, change the adolescent body image and self concept...Slow or rapid growth, unevenness of growth may affect an adolescent's total development," we heartily agreed.

When Toepfer said, "The realization that, as a group, emerging adolescent learners are distinctly different from either elementary or high school learners builds the logic that the middle unit of the school system must have an identity of its own," we warmly agreed.

Ironically, the strange marriage of acceptance of the developmental differences of transescents and the insistence on treating emerging adolescents the same educationally too often in the past continued to thwart realistic growth of appropriate programs.

Gertrude Noar in 1961, fifty years after the origin of the junior high school, stated, "The junior high schools, originally founded to meet the need for education on a level intermediate between elementary school and high school, have generally been accused of falling short of helping children for whom they are designed." Why are we still wrestling with this question? Bill Alexander, the great scholar of the middle school movement, states, "Between 1936-1966 a number of definitive longitudinal studies of the growth of boys and girls and of concomitant physical, social, and psychological phenomena were published with almost no perceptible impact on education."

We must ask ourselves why?

Louis Rubin offers further insight. Rubin says, "The public schools of this country have been, as an institution, extraordinarily resistant to change. School populations may vary drastically, the available knowledge and the means of communicating it may explode, a sexual revolution may begin, and a generation gap may develop, and still the schools go on as before, relevant or not, interesting or not, useful or not."

In my judgment, the singular most damaging reason for this dilemma is that the focal point for program has not been on the diverse uniqueness of the age group, but rather we have attempted to gerrymander students' diverse characteristics into a model of sameness and rigidity.

Our model for this age group has been a chronological age-graded model which has emphasized that all students are at a similar point in their maturational development and grow in yearly increments. This is tantamount to a football team playing the championship game on a baseball diamond. It is totally incompatible with the very basic nature of the group for which it serves. While we, without hesitation, accept the rationale of diversity, we have not at times in the past brought ourselves to develop programs which deviate from sameness. It just simply would not be educational.

I suggest that unless we reexamine the fundamental focus of schools in the middle, Gertrude Noar's criticism of 1960 will be just as appropriate in 1980 or 1990 as it is today. That unless we are willing to accept Havighurst's basic premise that the major lessons to be learned are physical and social we will, as Dr. Toepfer has stated, once again regress to the mean. The middle school move-ment has made remarkable strides, but like its predecessor, is now faced with the decision as to whether or not it will ultimately succeed. It still has the chance to continue to break the barrier and become a unique institution serving a unique group of students. Schools are dynamic – they must either go forward or backward.

The junior high faced with the same set of variables retreated to a program of sameness. It would be tragic for middle schools to repeat this pattern. How might we avoid this regression?

I would like to suggest we consider a different model for middle school education: the model of developmental age. The focal point for this model lies in the developmental differences of transescents rather than the qualities of sameness. By definition, developmental age refers to a youngster's physical and social maturational level. It is a concept widely accepted by other professions, such as medicine, which deal with youngsters in the 10 to 14 age span. It is a concept which is far more logical than the chronological-graded concept. Frank Faulkner, an eminent physician, succinctly points out its importance. Faulkner states:

> We are accustomed to describing an individual acquaintance by his chronological age. This factor is supposed to supply the final unmistakable clue. Yet, if the individual is described as a 13-year-old boy, human biologists are the first to be at a loss. Since there is such a very, very wide variation among normal children in the age of onset of the adolescent growth spurt, and since the period is one of such rapid growth, it is little wonder we are lost. The morphological, physiological, educational, and social implications of this difference are manifestly important In the field of human development, we must therefore consider another age process: developmental age.

Imagine physicians treating all 13-year-olds in the same manner simply because they are 13-year-olds. This approach would at best be foolish and at worst tragic. Obviously, the youngster must be medically treated in relation to maturational development; however, consider the model which middle school educators have often employed. Think about 13-year-olds for a moment. He may be 6 ft. 2 inches with a deep voice or 4 ft. 8 inches hoping to grow. She might be so awkward she trips going up stairs, or she might win an Olympic Gold Medal with a perfect 10.0 in parallel bar competition. He may be unable to read the comic page, or he might be solving problems in 10th grade geometry. She might be wearing mouth braces or competing in Miss Teen Age America. He might be curious, enthusiastic, and interested; or he might be turned off. He might be an alcoholic or a little leaguer.

It is these vast differences which make developmental age a viable concept. We have persisted, however, in stereotyping 13-year-olds. We eagerly departmentalize content, books, and students. We standardize test scores and declare any student not average or better a failure. We manipulate differences so they fit what adults say the typical 13-year-old should be.

At the risk of letting you hang in mid-air, I would like to conclude my remarks with a question and a challenge: What would a middle school be like if developmental age rather than the grade in school were the focal point of program development?

Further, I would offer a challenge. I challenge each of you to consider developmental age in relation to your middle school role.

I believe developmental age has the power to make the idea and implementation of the idea one and the same. ▶

Donald H. Eichhorn reflects...

Considering It All

T he middle school may be the most dynamic educational development since 1960. Its steady growth is indicative of its wide acceptance. The most recent figures available show nearly 10,000 middle schools (5-8, 6-8, and 7-8) with less than 1,500 junior high schools (7-9) remaining. In 1967, I theorized that youngsters in the 10-14 age group constituted a distinct stage of development and that this stage is occurring at an earlier time in biological development, and that current and former organizational models no longer adequately serve the transescent. Apparently that view is still valid.

The launching of Sputnik on October 4, 1957, created a national panic. It set off efforts to make major changes in American science, technology, and education. As I reflect on the emergence of the middle school and the many aspects of its transition, I would like to share my impressions of the tumultuous events which have molded the contemporary middle school. While this report is not fully comprehensive, I have attempted to present those incidents and persons that significantly shaped the pioneering efforts to improve education for the 10-14 year old student.

Impetus for change

Sputnik erroneously created a negative atmosphere in the nation. As Howard K. Smith stated in *Events Leading Up To My Death* (1996): "Now this spectacular Russian achievement highlighted every flaw in American society, including some that did not exist, and let loose an avalanche of self-criticism."

American education became an attack point for why the Soviets had won this first leg of "the race to space." A variety of new educational programs were created, and considerable time was spent in revamping academic programs. Since few teachers were prepared for imposed new programs, changing and modifying curriculum, especially in science and mathematics, consumed a large portion of their time. This, combined with societal changes brought the realization that the education of young adolescents needed improvement. It also prompted teacher education institutions to take a new look at that concern.

Other factors were also creating change. A profound, national cultural transformation began with the United States Supreme Court's ruling that segregation in the nation's schools was illegal. On May 17, 1954, the Supreme Court rendered its unanimous decision in *Brown v. The Board of Education*, concluding that "in the field of public education the doctrine of separate but equal has no place. Separate educational facilities are inherently unequal."

This landmark decision legally ended segregation and had an immense effect on American education and middle level education. Integration in the nation's schools called for considerable change. Minority groups, especially in urban areas, anticipated improved educational opportunities. In his national survey of middle schools Cuff (1965) noted: "In some cities integration was clearly a factor, as new attendance districts were made to cross old neighborhood boundaries and bring a diverse population into the intermediate grades" (p. 82-86).

New medical research confirmed that biological maturation was occurring at an earlier age and biological growth clearly impacted learning. Studies identified that young adolescents would benefit intellectually, emotionally, and socially from programs designed specifically for their age characteristics. I developed a label and a definition for this group of students who were leaving childhood but hadn't yet become fully adolescents. In *The Middle School* (1966) it was stated thusly:

> Transescence is the stage of development which begins prior to the onset of puberty and extends through the early stages of adolescence. Since puberty does not occur for all precisely at the same chronological age in human development, the transescent designation is based on the

many physical, social-emotional, and intellectual changes in body chemistry that appear prior to the time which the body gains a practical degree of stabilization over these complex pubescent changes. (p. 3)

Citizens response to change

The concept of middle level education was rooted in the nature of human growth and development. Therefore, it was bound to serve 10-14 year old students better. The concern then became to develop educational programs that were based on age characteristics. In communities such as Upper St. Clair, Pennsylvania, that decided to change from a junior high school to a middle school approach there was the concern that the middle school would simply implement the junior high school one year earlier. Resulting discussions between home and school eventually led to acceptance of the new concept. Initiating a model middle school involved many persons, both professional and non-professional. This coalition included parents, citizens, faculty members, school administrators, school board members, and representatives from higher education. The validity and purpose for a change emerged as planners learned more about the biological, intellectual, and social characteristics of the transescent students. A commitment from the school board, support from parents and the community, advocacy from the school administration, enthusiasm from the school principal, and a dedicated, innovative faculty were all necessary for success when putting the middle school philosophy into practice.

In that post-Sputnik era, professional staff members wrestled with alternative curriculum and instructional developments imposed upon them. Since few teachers were prepared for the middle school concept, faculties spent extensive time on in-service training studying the characteristics of this age group and planning appropriate curriculum.

Role of higher education

The leadership of the junior high school movement came largely from higher education. However, the middle school had a more "grass roots" emphasis. The middle school movement sought to build "theory into practice," something lacking in the earlier junior high school.

The foundation for the junior high school was laid by Charles W. Eliot, President of Harvard (1888-1918) and a prestigious National Education Association Committee. A small core of college professors presented their ideas in professional journals and committee reports. These early advocates proposed that the junior high school should be a lower level of the high school, not a separate level.

In the 1940s, William Gruhn and Harl Douglass developed a valuable list of functions of the junior high school which is still relevant. Then, William Alexander, a noted curriculum scholar, advanced the idea of a middle school and provided substance, prestige, and respect for the emerging movement in the 1960s. Forest Long, Gordon Vars, John Lounsbury, and Conrad F. Toepfer, Jr., who were first identified with the junior high school movement, contributed experience and visionary leadership as the junior high school movement merged with the middle school movement. These college and university professors began to articulate and work directly with practitioners in the field. As a result, a few teacher preparation institutions became involved with school districts in the kinds of partnerships noted earlier.

Despite its ultimate failings, the junior high had its bright spots. The development of the core curriculum in which subject lines were erased and students worked together to solve problems was an innovative approach to learning. Another contribution of the junior high school was the institution of exploratory courses. Most junior high schools did not become involved with the core program in part because of the lack of suitable teachers. Another concern effecting acceptance of the core curriculum was certification. In most states teachers could not teach out of their secondary field. Many core supporters see in the middle school a renewed emphasis on this instructional process. However, I believe that the interdisciplinary team concept may more effectively achieve the objectives of core curriculum.

Influence of professional organizations

A vital element in the growth of middle schools was the role played by major professional education organizations. One group that contributed to the early growth of middle schools was the Association for Supervision and Curriculum Development (ASCD). Many felt that the development of this new concept should take place within the nurturing structure of ASCD. At the time, ASCD provided an umbrella of services to those interested in middle schools. Since it was an organization of known quality, its support of the fledgling middle school movement was a vital contribution. In an effort to clarify the purposes and programs in the junior high school, the ASCD Commission on Secondary Curriculum prepared the position paper *The Junior High School We Need* (1961) and sponsored the 1962 study, *The Junior High School We Saw: One Day in the Eighth Grade.*

In 1969, Neil Atkins, Executive Secretary of ASCD appointed Donald Eichhorn as chairperson of the Emerging Adolescent Learner Council. Serving on the committee were Mary Compton, Bruce Howell, James Phillips, Thomas Sweeney, and Conrad F. Toepfer, Jr. The Council made two very important contributions to the middle school movement. The development of the quality multimedia presentation, *The Emerging Adolescent in the Middle Grades* (1973), and a monograph, *School of the Future—Now* (1972), edited by J. Galen Saylor, Chairman of ASCD's Continuous Learner Council. ASCD's sponsorship of the Continuous Education Council which consisted of the chairpersons of the Pre-School, Elementary, Emerging Adolescent Learner, and High School Councils. The acceptance of the Council of the Emerging Adolescent Learner as an equal partner with the other three councils substantially raised the middle school movement's prestige.

In 1974, the Executive Council of ASCD appointed a Working Group on the Emerging Adolescent Learner. Charles A. Dilg and Thomas E. Gatewood served as coordinators and guided committee members, Joseph C. Bondi, Jr., Robert Bumpus, and Inez Wood in developing a paper, *The Middle School We Need* (1974), that identified the rationale of the middle school and also addressed further issues of organization, administration, and curriculum.

Another national professional group with an interest in middle level education was the National Association of Secondary School Principals (NASSP). NASSP had earlier established a junior high school committee. To deal with the emerging administrative level organizational issues surrounding the middle school, NASSP established the Council on Middle Level Education under the leadership of George Melton, Deputy Executive Director of NASSP. Conrad F. Toepfer, Jr. chaired the Council, with Alfred Arth, J. Howard Johnston, and John H. Lounsbury serving as major members. They authored the document, *An Agenda for Excellence at the Middle Level* (1985) which examined 12 areas of schooling necessary for an exceptional middle school. This brief document was well received in the early post-*A Nation at Risk* years and was followed by several related documents. The council also conducted frontline conferences, sponsored three national shadow studies, developed a video, *Why a Middle School?* and otherwise provided leadership.

The National Association of Elementary School Principals (NAESP), the Association for Supervision and Curriculum Development, and NASSP all wanted the fledgling National Middle School Association to be part of their organizations. William Alexander suggested the four associations individually plan a mission statement, then convene to merge the four statements into a single working document. This effort failed when the various parties could not agree to meet. This resulted in NMSA's developing as an independent entity, and it has become the major professional organization involved with the middle school movement. From its small provincial start in 1973, NMSA has grown to be an influential national and international force in education. As it matured, it instituted a number of committees to further the development of various aspects of the movement such as research, publications, and teacher preparation.

The 1980 President of NMSA, John Swaim, appointed a committee with this charge: "Because the middle school concept has been implemented in a variety of different ways across the nation, the association felt that a clear and relatively complete statement was needed which would reflect the consensus views of the association regarding the essential elements of middle school education."

This committee included Alfred Arth serving as Coordinator, William Alexander, Charles Cherry, Conrad F. Toepfer, Jr., Gordon Vars, and Donald Eichhorn. John Lounsbury accepted the task of melding the sometimes conflicting views of the members into a consensus document. The resulting paper, *This We Believe* (1982), became a landmark document. It not only provided the rationale and definition of the middle school, it set the tone for middle schools for many years.

The direction established by *This We Believe* was, in effect, endorsed by the Carnegie Council on Adolescent Development in its widely distributed publication *Turning Points, Preparing American Youth for the 21st Century* (1989). This influential report described the conditions that plague young adolescents and set forth eight major recommendations for improving the education of young adolescents. The Carnegie Council subsequently launched its Middle Grade School State Policy Initiative that provided grants to various states to implement the recommendations.

Because of the tremendous growth of middle schools, new research, and accumulated experience, NMSA's Board of Trustees appointed a committee in 1994 to "revisit" the original position paper. John Arnold, Sherrel Bergmann, Barbara Brodhagen, Ross Burkhardt, Maria Garza-Lubeck Marion Payne, Sue Swaim, John Lounsbury, Gordon Vars, and Chris Stevenson served on this committee. The group's final report, adopted by the board, clarifies the rationale for middle level education and describes characteristics or conditions needed for an effective school. The content of this document, *This We Believe: Developmentally Responsive Middle Level Schools* (1995) closely parallels the original paper.

The National Middle School Association has maintained its singular purpose, real commitment, and enthusiasm. It continues to be an exciting and dynamic organization. Yet caution should be taken, for any large, rapidly expanding organization can become too political and lose its sense of mission.

Additional influences

There were a number of other events, organizations, or activities that had an impact on the development of the middle school movement and deserve to be recognized.

One early advocate of middle level education was the late Preston Brown, founder of **Educational Leadership Institute**. ELI sponsored and coordinated seminars around the nation which brought educators together to discuss and debate middle school issues. While not a member of the educational profession, Brown was always ready to contribute to the cause. His financial support of the ASCD multimedia presentation, *The Emerging Adolescent in the Middle Grades* (1973) was critical. He also supported middle schools by sponsoring research efforts, institutes, and workshops for school districts in addition to colleges and university workshops. In 1968, Educational Leadership Institute began to publish *Dissemination Services on the Middle School*, a monthly publication for middle school educators with Philip Pumerantz and Conrad C. Toepfer, Jr. as editors. Another important contribution by the ELI was the publication *Transescence: The Journal on Emerging Adolescent Education* which appeared in the spring of 1973 with Toepfer as editor. The journal developed into a comprehensive and challenging publication when there were few materials available.

The initiation of state or regional leagues or organizations was another unique development that encouraged the development of middle schools. These groups, some of which pre-dated NMSA, offered assistance on a state or regional basis to middle school supporters. The National Middle School Association itself evolved out of the Midwest Middle School Association. (Glenn Maynard, professor at Kent State University, was a key person in the development of the MMSA and in the transition to NMSA.) Other early leagues were the Florida, New England, and Western Pennsylvania Leagues.

The National Resource Center for Middle Schools, created and directed by Robert Malinka, played a critical role in the early development of middle schools. With virtually no professional literature on the middle school available, few exemplary schools to visit, few "experts" to call on for assistance, this facility located in the Indianapolis Public Schools became something of a public vertical file, a clearinghouse for information on scheduling, advisory programs, interdisciplinary teaming, and other topics. A model of cooperation and collaboration, the center's services were of inestimable value in the 60s and 70s.

The Center of Education for Young Adolescence at the University of Wisconsin, Platteville, is dedicated to improving the middle level students' educational experiences. Its annual summer seminars gave considerable impetus to implementing middle school practices. The workshops place heavy emphasis on creative curriculum planning and take-home projects. Started by Robert Shockley and continuing under the direction of Robert Stone, this institute has been a model other states have followed.

In 1972, a significant middle level field project was conducted in the Decatur, Alabama, school system. Designed to prepare a school district for instituting middle schools while implementing racial integration, the project involved the University of Alabama as a partner. Two newly constructed middle schools were built in Decatur on an open space concept. In each of the two schools there were three houses of 500 students. A part of the project was a six-week graduate course taught by Donald Eichhorn. The local plan was designed by Robert Bumpus, Decatur's Director of Curriculum, who conducted and coordinated the various local elements. The University of Alabama's field representative, Dr. Gerald Firth, directed the interaction between the University and the Decatur School System. Eichhorn acted as a liaison for all the groups. The exceptional morale, enthusiasm and *esprit de corps* of those involved with the project assured a positive accomplishment of its purposes. The two middle schools quickly became early models of excellence and were visited by hundreds of educators and administrators.

The international growth of the middle school movement was encouraged by George J. Pimenides. As principal of the American International Community Middle School in Athens, Greece, Pimenides guided his staff in developing an outstanding program.

Traveling to the United States to broaden his knowledge about middle schools, Pimenides attended annual NMSA conferences from 1975 until his death in 1991. The exceptional school that Pimenides developed inspired the beginning and continuing development of international middle schools. The first International Middle Level School Conference held in Brussels, Belgium, in January, 1987, led to the further development of the European League of Middle Schools.

Research

In October, 1969, the Boyce Medical Study was initiated. It involved 494 sixth, seventh, and eighth grade students at the Boyce Middle School in suburban Upper St. Clair, Pennsylvania. This unique study was a joint effort between the medical and educational professions. Medically, the main purpose of the study directed by Dr. Alan Drash of the Children's Hospital in Pittsburgh was to establish data on the level of biological maturation of middle level students and to assess their general health. Educationally, the study I directed was to develop an educational model that reflected the information derived.

The data led Eichhorn to advocate "developmental age grouping" rather than traditional grouping based on age and grade level. Five units of approximately 120 were developed to group students according to their developmental age group: (1) pre-pubescent, (2) pubescent, (3) early adolescent-a, (4) early adolescent -b, and (5) adolescent.

This grouping pattern conflicted with the traditional curriculum and instructional components. Therefore, the Boyce faculty had to restructure its educational plan. Under the leadership of the Principal, James Welsh, the Boyce School opened during the 1969-1970 school year. Over the next five years, the results of these innovative changes were extraordinarily positive. For example, during this time period, there was a five month increase in achievement scores in the Pennsylvania Department of Education's Educational Assessment Test and ranked first among the state's schools on the achievement portion of the E.Q. test. The study made a direct impact on grouping procedures at the middle level. It was proven at Boyce Middle School that developmental age grouping was a viable approach and had the potential to improve educational programs for the transescent learner.

As suspected, the general health of the study group was excellent. However, the medical team was surprised to find an abnormally high level of cholesterol in blood and urine samples of eight per cent of the students. At the time, the link between high cholesterol and heart disease was just beginning to be accepted. Medically, Drash indicated that the Boyce study formed the basis for several subsequent medical investigations pertaining to this age group.

In 1989, William Alexander and C. Kenneth McEwin published their study, *Schools in the Middle: Status and Progress.* This statistical project encompassed two decades of research involving virtually all aspects of middle level education. The study partially followed the original national project conducted by Alexander in 1968. Subsequently, Ken McEwin, Tom Dickinson, and Doris Jenkins surveyed middle schools in 1993 using an instrument that incorporated questions from the 1968 and 1988 studies along with many new questions. Their report, *America's Middle Schools: Practices and Progress—A 25 Year Perspective* (1996), provided needed data on the extent of various programs and characteristics and the progress made over the past 25 years.

The shadow studies by Lounsbury and his associates have provided insights into the daily school lives of middle students. This unique study technique was first utilized by Lounsbury and Marani in 1962 when seventh and eighth graders in junior high school were "shadowed" (*The Junior High School We Saw: One Day in the Eighth Grade*, ASCD, 1964). Nationally, on a given day, observers would follow a randomly selected student throughout the school day, recording at five-minute intervals the nature of his/her activities. In 1977, under the sponsorship of the NMSA, a seventh grade shadow study project was conducted to provide data that would aid in assessing the middle school movement. In the publication, *The Middle School Profile: A Day in the Seventh Grade* (1980), Lounsbury, Marani, and Compton concluded that the state of the middle was:

...clearly improved – not excellent, perhaps not even very good, but noticeably better. The middle school today, as one would expect, is still very much of a mixed bag. There are hundreds of middle schools operating that are wholly departmentalized, homogeneously grouped, subject matter centered and featuring interscholastic athletics. These schools display all that typified what became the typical junior high school. On the other hand, there are many middle schools that operate in open spaces, that feature real team teaching, extensive exploratory programs, adviser-advisee arrangements, and nearly all the theoretically acceptable practices. The vast majority, of course, are somewhere in between and cluster around the middle. (p. 65)

The National Association of Secondary School Principals subsequently sponsored additional shadow studies. Lounsbury and J. Howard Johnston directed the ninth grade study, *How Fares the Ninth Grade* (1985), and the sixth grade study, *Life in the Three Sixth Grades* (1988). Under the direction of Lounsbury and Donald C. Clark, eighth graders were shadowed on March 8, 1989. One fundamental finding in all of these studies was the importance of the teacher. Lounsbury and Clark state in *Inside Grade Eight: From Apathy to Excitement* (1990): "It is naïve to assume significant changes can be made simply by changing schedules, textbooks, or courses, and bypassing the personal growth of teachers."

Another study that impacted the middle school's instructional agenda was conducted by Herman Epstein and Conrad Toepfer, Jr. This research, termed "brain growth periodization," suggested that during pubescence brain growth slows to a significant degree. The results of these findings challenged the belief that the majority of students attained Piaget's level of formal operations between the ages of ten and fourteen. Toepfer (1982) summarized Epstein's findings:

Epstein's data suggest that the human brain grows in a periodic or stagewise fashion in which growth "spurts"

alternate with times of low growth. His findings indicate
that intervals of greater brain growth occur somewhere
between the ages of 3 to 10 months, 2 to 4 years, 6 to 8
years, 10 to 12 years and 14 to 16 years. Periods of lesser
growth in the brain are believed to occur somewhere
between the ages 10 months and 2, 4 and 6, 8 and 10 and
12 to 14 years. (p. 657)

This theory sparked discussion and debate throughout the nation.
While the concept of brain growth periodization remains controver-
sial, Epstein and Toepfer's work will continue to challenge current
learning dogma. Based on longitudinal study of British young adolescents by Adey and Shayer (1994), Epstein and Toepfer presented their
latest findings at the 1996 NMSA annual conference.

Challenges

As it has emerged, the middle school movement has provided a
growing foundation for creatively advancing the education of 10-14
year old students. In 1971 I stated:

Possibly, the greatest challenge to the future of middle
schools is the willingness of those committed to creatively
pioneer programs designed specifically for the early adolescent learner. While in many cases, these programs have yet
to emerge, the future worth of this level demands that they
be created. The promise of middle level education lies in its
great potential. It presents educators with immense possibilities. If educators are content merely to apply the inadequate approach of the past, middle schools will simply go
the way of former organizations. If, however, educators are
prepared to study the characteristics and needs of this
unique student and initiate imaginative approaches to
program development, the promise of the future for middle
school educators can be fulfilled. (Saylor [Ed.], 1972b)

As middle level educators face the future, continuing challenges
need to be addressed. These obstacles may be difficult to resolve but

the need to deal with them is vital and urgent. The following are concerns that merit constant attention:

To maintain the basic rationale of the middle school. The concept which governs middle level education is that curriculum, instruction, and activity programs be directed at the students' characteristics. Difficulties arrive when designed programs are out of synch with the level of student maturation. If a student's cognition lies in concrete operations, he/she should not be placed in a program which requires abstract thinking. Past instructional schedules often violated this principle of readiness. When student growth and development are reflected in creating programs, successful learning results.

To develop programs that educate and prepare students for a rapidly changing technological world. Although students will need to earn a living and master technologies that quickly become obsolete, the temptation to over-accelerate learning could be a mistake and should be avoided. Students need to build a cognitive foundation before they can theorize and conceptualize in higher levels of learning. Incorporating technology in the curriculum should be done with the learners' characteristics in mind. As stated in *An Agenda for Excellence at the Middle Level* (NASSP, 1985).

> Because we cannot teach them all they need to know, we must teach them how to learn and how to adjust their lives to the changes that will surround them. To do this, we must provide high quality intellectual climates in our middle level schools and foster the development of adaptive skills that our students can use throughout their lives. (p. 1-2)

To expand the role of the home and community in the schools. Early advocates of the middle school believed that parents and other citizens in the community should be encouraged to participate in school programs. NMSA strongly advocated that parents and families be actively involved and included. The presence of parents and other community adult members is needed to affirm to students that not just teachers have an interest in their educational potential and progress.

To seek creative ways to confront home, school, and community problems. There is a need to identify problems confronting students and to utilize the resources of home, school, and community to solve them. The downward drift of youths' values is of great concern. The physical, biological, and mental aspects of 10-14 year old youngsters make them particularly vulnerable to violent crime, teenage pregnancies, casual sexual practices with attendant sexually transmitted diseases, and the use of harmful substances. Educators and the schools are in a difficult situation which can only be ameliorated through education, guidance, and innovative programs supported by the community.

To use the great potential of the present program. As the middle school emerged, it developed a number of functional practices that have potential. Among them is the concept of teaming. By inventively building upon this concept and other related middle level practices, the possibilities for significantly improved and different educational experiences for young adolescents are unlimited.

To encourage teacher preparation institutions to become involved with middle level learning. The teacher's role will need to be greatly altered and expanded. New and varied teaching techniques as well as different perceptions of the teacher's and school's role will need to be acquired. Many higher education institutions have successfully initiated innovative middle level teacher preparation curriculum. It is essential that more colleges and universities emphasize in their teacher preparation courses the need for specialized preparation for those who wish to teach in the middle level.

Conclusion

The present status of the middle school movement is exciting. Today, the middle level has finally gained acceptance as a distinctive, separate division of education. The vast majority of middle level schools are composed of grades 6, 7, and 8. Progress continues to be made in instructional programs that are developmentally appropriate. By following a proven rationale and defining a statement of beliefs, middle level educators have created exciting schools for the "student in the middle."

There is some of apprehension, however, as we approach the twenty-first century. Daily, science and technology change our lives, especially in the area of communications. Using a computer, our students can go to school with and learn from children in distant lands. Providing the machinery for inter-global education will be a challenge to school planners who are constantly confronted with changes in economic patterns. Budget limitations, pressure groups, and the heavy hand of tradition all present difficulties now and in the immediate future.

It hardly seems possible that it has been thirty-two years since *The Middle School* (1966) was published. Over the years, the growth of the middle school movement evolved due to the knowledge, expertise, experience, and insight of many dedicated educators who envisioned the need and the potential for this level of instruction. The result has been a steady revamping of one area of American schooling. It has been my privilege to have had a part in this significant development. ❯

References

Alexander, W., & McEwin, C. K. (1989). *Schools in the middle: Status and progress.* Columbus, OH: National Middle School Association.

Beane, J.A., Toepfer, C.F., Jr., & Alessi, S.J., Jr. (1986). *Curriculum planning and development.* Newton, MA: Allyn and Bacon.

Brown v. Board of Educ., 347 U.S. 483 (1954).

Carnegie Council on Adolescent Development. (1989). *Turning points: Preparing American youth for the 21st century.* New York: Carnegie Corporation.

Council on Middle Level Education. (1985). *An agenda for excellence at the middle level.* Reston, VA: National Association of Secondary School Principals.

Council on Middle Level Education. (1987). *Developing a mission statement for the middle level schools.* Reston, VA: National Association of Secondary School Principals.

Cuff, W.A. (1967). Middle schools on the march. Reston, VA: *Bulletin of the National Association of Secondary School Principals,* 82-86.

David, R.J. (Ed.). (1995). *Eichhorn: The early years in middle level education.* Pittsburgh, PA: Pennsylvania Middle School Association.

DeVita, J.C., Pumerntz, P.W., Leighton. (1970). *The effective middle school.* West Nyack, NY: Parker Publishing Co, Inc.

Eichhorn, D.H. (1967, December). *Rationale for emergence: A look at the middle school.* Paper presented at the Middle School Conference, University of Pittsburgh, PA. (Reprinted in R.J. David [Ed.], *Eichhorn: The early years in middle level education,*1995, pp. 13-32, Pittsburgh, PA: Pennsylvania Middle School Association).

Eichhorn, D.H. (1972a). The Boyce Medical Study: Educational dimensions of the emerging adolescent learner in the middle grades. In N. Atkins & P. Pumermantz (Eds.), Multimedia presentation. Springfield, MA: Association for Supervision and Curriculum Development and Educational Leadership Institute

Eichhorn, D. H. (1972b). The emerging adolescent school of the future – now. In J. Galen Saylor (Ed.) *The school of the future – now.* Washington, DC: Association for Supervision and Curriculum Development.

Eichhorn, D.H. (1980). Toward adolescence: The middle school years.*The School. Offprint from the Seventy-ninth Yearbook of the National Society for the Study of Education..* Chicago, IL: The National Society for the Study of Education.

Gatewood, T.E., & Dilg, C. (1975). *The middle school we need.* Washington, DC: Association for Supervision and Curriculum Development.

Johnson, M. (Ed.). (1980). *Toward adolescence, The middle school years.* Seventy-ninth yearbook of the National Society for the Study of Education, Part I. Chicago, IL: The National Society for the Study of Education.

Lounsbury, J.H., & Vars, G. (1978). *A curriculum for the middle school years.* New York: Harper and Row, Publishers.

Lounsbury, J.H., Marani, J., & Compton, M. (1980). *The middle school in profile: A day in the seventh grade.* Columbus, OH: National Middle School Association.

Lounsbury, J. H. (1984). *Middle school education: As I see it.* Columbus, OH: National Middle School Association.

Lounsbury, J.H., & Johnston, J. H. (1985). *How fares the ninth grade?* Reston, VA: National Association of Secondary School Principals.

Lounsbury, J.H. & Johnston J. H. (1988). *Life in the three sixth grades.* Reston, VA: National Association of Secondary School Principals.

Lounsbury, J.H., & Clark, D.C. (1990). *Inside grade eight: From apathy to excitement.* Reston, VA: National Association of Secondary School Principals.

National Education Association. (1899).*Journal of proceedings and addresses.* Los Angeles, CA: Author.

National Middle School Association. (1982). *This we believe.* Columbus, OH: Author.

National Middle School Association (1995). *This we believe: Developmentally responsive middle level schools:* Columbus, OH: Author.

Smith, H.K. (1996). *Events leading up to my death.* New York: St. Martin's Press.

Steer, D.R. (Ed.). (1980). *The emerging adolescent characteristics and educational implications.* Columbus, OH: National Middle School Association.

Transescence: The Journal on Emerging Adolescent Education, Vol. XXI, Number 1 (1993). Conrad C. Toepfer, Jr. (Ed.).Springfield, MA: Educational Leadership Institute.

III

John H. Lounsbury

The four articles I selected set forth my views about intermediate education during the early years. The first three are focused exclusively on the junior high school and were published in March 1956, January 1960, and December 1960, all before the term middle school was advanced by the late William Alexander. The last one is much more recent, 1977, and was one of the first articles I wrote dealing exclusively with the middle school itself. It was included in the first NMSA-published monograph.

These writings were published over a period of twenty-one years and range from as far back as forty-two years ago to as recently as nineteen years ago. They may offer some historical perspective on middle level education and have inherent interest to contemporary educators.

JOHN H. LOUNSBURY

What Has Happened to the Junior High School?

Published in *Educational Leadership*, March, 1956

O riginally conceived as a downward extension of secondary education, the modern junior high school – despite its label – now appears to be increasingly an upward extension of elementary education.

In the United States, the junior high school is about as old as the automobile. Shortly after Duryea chugged down the streets of Springfield, Massachusetts, in 1893 in his first automobile, a new intermediate school was erected to house the pupils of the seventh and eighth grades in the Richmond, Indiana of 1895. But the beginnings of high production in the automobile industry did not come until the years 1909-1912. And the real beginnings of the junior high school movement in America were not until 1909-10 when Columbus, Ohio, and Berkeley, California organized junior high schools. Mass production of junior high schools followed as Grand Rapids, Michigan; Los Angeles, California: Concord, New Hampshire; Evansville, Indiana; and a growing host of other school systems joined the junior high school procession.

Like the Model T, the junior high school vehicle got under way auspiciously and with considerable fanfare. Educators quickly climbed aboard what seemed to them an excellent way of correcting numerous ills evident in the American school system during the early 1900s. Riders came aboard hoping to achieve one or another of the early functions of the junior high school. Included among these early purposes were:

1. Effecting economy in time through earlier offering of college preparatory subjects, the elimination of duplication, promotion by subjects, and departmental teaching.

2. Improving articulation between elementary and secondary education by introducing an intermediate step and gradually inaugurating the elective system.

3. Improving the noticeably poor holding power of the schools and reducing the heavy number of failures and repeaters by new and richer content, vocational work, departmental teaching, and other features.

4. Making possible a program better suited to the nature of early adolescents by providing needed special facilities, by organizing vocational training for those who left school early, and by homogeneously grouping the pupils to help take care of their individual differences. A program better suited to the early adolescents could also be made possible by segregating them from the younger children and the sophisticated older adolescents to the benefit of all three groups, and by providing guidance services to assist with the many kinds of problems which accompany this age level.

5. Providing for exploration by offering short-term or try-out courses, by testing, counseling, and exploratory work to discover pupils' interests and abilities, and by offering vocational orientation work.

During the 'tens and 'twenties of this century, both the automobile market and the junior high school movement boomed. Some thought the infant educational institution to be a veritable cure for all ills. At the annual NEA meeting in 1916, one educator declared enthusiastically that the junior high school was "sweeping the country." By 1920 many informed professional men were crusading for the junior high school. Surveys recommended it in community after community.

During the decade 1920-30, the number of junior high schools underwent amazing growth. In 1920 there were about 100 separate junior high schools. By 1930 there were 1,842. From only about one-half of one percent of the secondary enrollment in 1920, the figure rose sharply to 20 percent by 1930. Articles on this uniquely American school flooded the professional periodicals. By 1930 more than twenty-five books on the junior high school had appeared.

However, the onrush of the junior high school vehicle slowed down during the 'thirties and 'forties. Though the number of junior high schools continued to increase somewhat, some of the zeal characteristic of the proponents in the early years diminished.

JOHN H. LOUNSBURY

Between 1931 and 1947, only two books on the junior high school
appeared. A corresponding decrease of magazine articles may be
noted. Some educators began saying that the junior high school
movement was largely a failure. One predicted that the junior high
school would "gradually pass from the picture as a separate
school." The junior high school vehicle, which once rode heavily
laden with eager educators, seemed to be losing some speed and
many riders.

Yet an educational Nostradamus might well predict that the junior
high school years will become an increasingly important school
segment in the next decade. He might base his prophecy on such
signs as the following:

1. The recognition by the United States Office of Education of a
"currently growing interest in the junior high school." On the basis
of this conviction, the office has launched a number of projects.
These include the holding last February of a National Conference of
Junior High Schools, and the publication of a number of circulars,
bulletins, and bibliographies dealing with the junior high school.

2. The authorization and inauguration of a three-year study on
the education of young adolescents by the Southern States Work
Conference.

3. The recent study conducted by the New York State Education
Department. This comprehensive and cooperative effort resulted in
publication of *A Design for Improving Early Secondary Education in
New York State.*

4. The increased activities of the National Association of Secondary School Principals in this area. This association, incidentally, has
continuously both reported and supported the development of the
junior high school movement. The organization encouraged the
study of the junior high school even during the years when it
seemed to be an educational orphan.

5. The activities of the California Association of School Administrators which developed a handbook for junior high school educators and, more recently, has produced a color film, *The Junior High
School Story.*

6. The mounting number of recent publications dealing with the junior high school. Included in this number is *Junior High School Trends,* by Leonard V. Koos, one of the early guiding lights in the movement. Another contribution is *The Junior High School – Today and Tomorrow,* by Gertrude Noar, for many years a capable junior high school principal. Gruhn and Douglass have just revised their book, *The Modern Junior High School.*

7. The interest of frontier curriculum groups, particularly the Association for Supervision and Curriculum Development, in the core curriculum. The ASCD recently published the booklets, *Developing Programs for Young Adolescents* and *Preparation of Core Teachers for Secondary Schools.* The core curriculum is found much more frequently at the junior high school level than at the senior high school level. The well-known 1950 study by Grace Wright of the United States Office of Education revealed that 86 percent of the core-type programs existing were in grades 7, 8, and 9. A study by the present writer involving 8 percent of all the junior high schools in the country shows that 12 percent of these randomly selected junior high schools are using a "problem-centered block of time." One-third of the junior high schools practice "correlation of two or more subjects" and an additional one-third report a "fusion of two or more subjects."

A new model

The junior high school in America may be undergoing a renaissance. This neglected area may soon be back in the limelight. The "forgotten teaching area" may be overlooked no longer.

Perhaps educators should look carefully at the present model of the junior high school. The vehicle proved to be more than a strange experiment. As it was refined it proved to be a sound and sturdy conveyance for the middle school travels, more comparable to the modern station wagon. It has served well as a testing ground for experimentation with newer practices. It is more functional than other secondary school models. There are reports of more improvements and increased production in the years ahead.

Discerning educators will quickly notice that this year's model is substantially different from earlier versions. This institution is no Model T. The modern model does not fly the banner of departmentalization. The large chart, setting forth the supposedly "unique" functions of the junior high school is not in sight. The slogan, "Economize time with a junior high," no longer appears in the advertising.

Some familiar faces are missing among the riders on the junior high school station wagon today. Lost are most of the educators concerned with dropouts. Today they are working over at the senior high school. It also rides without the vocational educators. They too are working at the senior high school, and some are at the junior college. The proponents of ability grouping are not nearly so numerous among the goodly company. Supporters of promotion by subjects in a completely departmentalized structure are few and far between. Educators championing earlier college preparation are conspicuous by their absence.

Despite these losses, the station wagon is full. New riders have come aboard. The core curriculum advocates are especially well represented. Psychologists are comfortably seated. (But in their briefcases they no longer carry the works of G. Stanley Hall, who characterized the adolescents as "a new being" and whose psychological disciples crowded the earliest models. The psychologists today are carrying books on human growth from the womb to the tomb.) Industrial arts men who emphasize general education have taken the seats of the vocational educators. And look again. Some elementary educators are aboard. Though the junior high school was originally conceived and carried out as a downward extension of secondary education, the modern junior high school – despite its label – now appears to be increasingly an upward extension of elementary education.

Many of the older riders are left. Some have been loyal since 1910 when the experimental models got under way. Those concerned with reducing failures and avoiding excessive retentions still ride. The supporters of education for democratic citizenship have an established seat. Guidance-minded teachers continue to travel.

No calliope, blaring brassily, follows the junior high school vehicle down the street today. The riders do not seem to be crusaders for the junior high school trademark. We hear less discussion of the importance and virtue of "separateness."

After all, there is not much sense in continuing a crusade after the crusade has gained its goals. The battle to reorganize secondary education has largely been won. The fad has become a fact. Four year high schools now make up less than half of the secondary schools. United States Office of Education figures, derived from the 1951-52 Biennial Survey reveal that only 18 of the 48 states still have 50 percent or more of their secondary schools organized as four-year or regular high schools. Maryland has no four year schools left. The District of Columbia has its entire secondary school population housed in either junior or senior high schools. Seven other states have 15 percent or less of their secondary schools remaining as four year high schools.

From the standpoint of enrollment the victory of the junior high school or reorganization movement is even more certain. Of every 100 secondary pupils, only 25 are enrolled in four-year high schools. Forty are on the registers of either junior or senior high schools. The remaining 35 are entered in junior-senior and undivided five- and six-year high schools. With new buildings being erected and consolidation continuing, there are indications that reorganized secondary schools will become even more prevalent.

The present model of the junior high school has a different destination. It heads for a good educational program for young adolescents. The modern riders are less concerned about particular grade organizations and administrative arrangements. They believe there are many "roads to Rome."

Those who ride the modern model in the junior high school movement look like a competent group. They seem to know where they are going. For maps, they have research and techniques denied their pioneering predecessors. They now have considerable experience under their belts. They are aware of changes in the role of the junior high school – changes which have grown out of shifts in the cultural context and modifications in generally accepted psychological and educational theory.

The riders welcome additional passengers as the junior high school does seem to have been neglected by many in the decade just past. And supporters of the modern junior high school vehicle are certainly needed, for the education of young adolescents is a perplexing and important problem. With the goal of a good educational program for early adolescents as the destination, the junior high school vehicle seems to be going somewhere today. ▶

What Keeps Junior from Growing Up?

Published in *Clearing House*, January, 1960

T he outcome of the junior high school movement is no longer in question. The educational infant of the 1910s has become the standard institution for young adolescents in America. More than three-fourths of all secondary pupils are now enrolled in some type of reorganized secondary school, one-fifth of them in the approximately 4,000 separate junior high schools. Within a decade perhaps many of the remaining four-year high schools will have passed from the educational scene, for the well established trend to reorganize is undergoing a speed-up. Eight-four advocates are few and far between and eight-four practitioners are dwindling. But junior hasn't really grown up.

Junior-high-school education lacks prestige

A first obstacle to junior's adulthood is the lack of prestige which accompanies junior high school education. This condition is a very difficult one to attack or change, but the damage that is done because it has been so is not hard to see. The lack of status often is apparent when a new teacher is hired and placed in the junior high school with the promise that he can have the first appropriate vacancy in the senior high. At the worst, he is told, he will only have to stay in the junior high a year or two. A newspaper refers to the transfer of the junior high principal to the senior high as a "promotion." Financially, of course, it may be a promotion, for senior highs are generally larger schools. This difference in status is readily observable, however, whether or not it shows up in the pay check. Quite often, educators themselves as well as the lay public in general have not accepted the junior high school as a distinctive level. To many, it's still an "in-between," a "stepchild." This almost unconscious attitude of inferiority has tremendous influence in dozens of decisions.

Inadequate facilities and housing

The buildings which house junior high schools have seldom been built as junior high schools. Quite typically they are moved into the old high-school building when the favored institution takes over the community's new pride, the modern senior high-school building. So the junior high school sets up shop in the old building and, from the beginning, is saddled with the obsolescence and limitations which seemed to require a new school. Or perhaps it moves into a former elementary building which is too small, has no gymnasium, no shop or homemaking facilities.

This matter of housing is an obstacle which lately has been given increasing attention. The post World War II years have seen a tremendous number of schools planned and built as junior high schools. Future prospects are quite bright too. Recent issues of such periodicals as the *Nation's Schools* contain numerous descriptions of functionally and carefully designed junior high schools. Many new urban junior high schools, even though they are large, are so designed that the total school is physically divided into a number of "little schools."

Lack of standards and regulations

A third block to growth and improvement is the absence of adequate standards, regulations, and policies for the junior high-school level. Because it lacked status the junior high school has had to shift for itself. It grew up with little or no preliminary planning and supervision on the state level. Some districts still require junior high schools to report their attendance on two separate forms. The ninth grade figures go on the high school form and the seventh and eighth grade figures on the regular elementary forms. Separate budgets are sometimes required and allotments come in two different pieces. The senior high schools expect a Carnegie unit accounting for ninth grade work, but are not concerned with the work in the other two grades. The junior high school often exists, then, in a subservient state because local boards and state departments have not accepted it as a unit and encouraged its growth by altering their reporting forms, their financial allotment formulas, and their graduation requirements, or by establishing clear policies to cover the junior high school. In the absence of clear standards many schools have simply called themselves junior high schools in order to take advantage of such a designation. One western state, for instance, allots 1/5 more money per A.D.A. unit for junior high schools than for elementary schools. Unless standards accompany such allotments, financially pinched administrators may take advantage of the provision.

An unfortunate label

Another block to the maturity of the junior high school is the institution's name. As we look back over the movement from our vantage point of fifty years, we can see how unfortunate it was that the name "junior high" caught on. Of course, it did describe best what many of the first junior high schools were supposed to be. Yet a number of the earliest reorganized schools, including the very first one, were called "intermediate schools." This is probably preferable, though not perfect. So long as junior high schools are called junior high schools, they will have a difficult time achieving the prestige and status due them. Even a completely unbiased stranger to American education would likely form a subservient concept of the middle institution when he was told the names of our school units. In our culture especially, the word "junior" conveys immaturity. Now forty-nine years old, junior deserves a handle which better conveys the acceptance he has earned in our school system. This is a factor to be reckoned with despite the old saw that a rose by any other name smells just as sweet.

Lack of specially trained teachers

A fifth obstacle is the lack of teachers who are specifically trained for junior high school work. Only a handful of the hundreds of institutions that train teachers have a definite program for prospective junior high school people. An occasional summer school course in the junior high school is about all most of the college catalogues have contained. The preparation of junior high-school teachers is the "blind spot" in teacher education. While the colleges are partially at fault for this state of affairs, they are by no means completely responsible for it. Certification requirements are vague, overlapping, or nonexistent with respect to junior-high-school teachers. Typically an elementary or secondary certificate will permit one to work in a junior high. Only the secondary certificates of Vermont and the District of Columbia will not authorize one to teach in grades 7 and 8. Only about six other states issue junior high-school certificates, and some of these states have no really distinctive requirements. It appears then that the same subject specialization which is required of high school teachers is the major criterion for employment as a junior high school instructor. No particular professional preparation is expected in most cases which might give junior high teachers a full understanding of the needs, characteristics, and interests of early adolescents or the functions and development of the junior high school.

This, too, is a stumbling block which is now receiving some attention. Two of the states which have separate certificates recently inaugurated them. Many universities and colleges are now planning programs for the preparation of junior high school teachers. For the past several years a committee of the National Association of Secondary School Principals has conducted a survey of summer junior high school offerings. The number of such courses and workshops has increased considerably each year. Forward-looking school systems, however, are not waiting for the colleges to turn out fully prepared junior high teachers. Through in-service programs they are developing the needed competencies and understandings. For instance, in one midwestern city all junior high people are given instruction in the teaching of reading.

Junior, then, is handicapped by several situations or conditions as he struggles for full maturity. Real progress, however, can be noted and most of the problems will be overcome sooner or later, for junior, like his human counterpart, will grow up! ❱

Reprinted with permission of the Helen Dwight Reid Educational Foundation. Published by Heldref Publications, 1319 Eighteenth St., N.W., Washington, D.C. 20036-1802. Copyright © 1960 (V. 34, No. 5, pp. 301-303)

How the Junior High School Came to Be

Published in *Educational Leadership*, December, 1960

When Indianola Junior High School of Columbus, Ohio, opened in September of 1909, it was the first school to be specifically called a junior high school. Now, 51 years later, there are 5000 schools labeled junior high schools. Another 3000 are called senior high schools. Today, less than 6000 schools remain as traditional four-year high schools in 8-4 systems. The reorganized secondary schools, that is those that deviate from a four-year high school following an eight year elementary school, now make up 76 percent of the 24,000 secondary schools and enroll 82 percent of the eleven million secondary pupils.[1]

The movement to reorganize secondary education has certainly come a long way since Charles W. Eliot first suggested the possibility of reorganization in 1888. Between that date and 1909-1910, the reorganization movement was confined primarily to the talking stage. Then the appearance of a number of new intermediate institutions moved reorganization into the experimental stage. During the 1920s the junior high school partners in the reorganization movement were rapidly growing educational innovations. In the 1930s the junior high school, the senior high school, and the combination junior-senior high school became accepted members of the American school family. By the close of the 1950s the separate junior high school followed by the separate senior high school, had become the predominant pattern of secondary school organization in the United States. Together these institutions enrolled 50 percent of the secondary school population.

The movement centering around the junior high school, though already successful, is still a relatively young movement: Yet the span

[1]The figures given are 1959 estimates based on preliminary data as reported by the United States Office of Education in the May 1960 issue of *School Life*, p. 10-12.

of this intermediate institution's existence is long enough so that the history of the high school movement can be viewed with reasonable objectivity. And it is appropriate to give some attention to the institution's historical development, for our understanding of the present and our vision for the future are incomplete without a knowledge of how and why the junior high school came to be.

Multiple causes

As might be expected, a number of causes underlie the development and expansion of the junior high school movement. Things are seldom as simple as they seem at first glance. The glib quick answer of a pseudo-expert satisfies only those who know less. A scholar sees deeper, notes interrelationships, and only hesitantly draws conclusions. With reservation then, the factors which have helped to bring about the tremendous growth of the American junior high school can be considered.

"What is the present after all, but a growth out of the past?" asked Walt Whitman. His question with its built-in answer was well stated, for institutions and major events never spring up independent of time and place. They evolve from and are shaped by the ongoing society. The junior high school is a prime example, for it truly grew out of the times and has continued to shift with the times. The whole history of the junior high school movement is closely paralleled to the social, economic, and political developments of the half-century which encompasses its life. The reader may be expecting some more spectacular statements regarding how the junior high came to be, but that is really the essence of it. The junior high school was initiated, developed, and grew because a variety of factors, all of which related to the times and existing educational theory and practice supported it in one way or another.

The junior high school did not grow simply because college presidents in the 1890s wanted secondary schools to speed up and improve college preparation. Nor did the junior high school develop because several national committees issued influential reports which supported reorganization proposals in the period 1892 to 1918. The junior high school did not grow because educators were seeking a solution to the appallingly high rate of dropouts and retardation as revealed by the pioneer studies of Ayers, Strayer, and Thorndike. The junior high school did not come about simply because many educators were levying criticisms on the existing system with its all-too-evident ills and shortcomings. Nor did the junior high school start because psychologists, like G. Stanley Hall, supported special institutions as being better able to cope with the "new beings" early adolescent were thought to be.

The junior high school did not grow because educators aspired to put into practice more completely new understandings of individual differences which the psychologists were clarifying through their research in the 1910s. The junior high school did not grow simply because it afforded an outlet for the strong reaction against traditional education led by noted educational philosophers. The junior high school was not caused by the fact that the growing masses of immigrants and urban dwellers required a more extensive type of citizenship education. The junior high school was not created because the many who never reached the later years of high school needed vocational training. The junior high school did not come to its current position because it was a good solution to the school building shortage caused by World War I and again by World War II.

No, the junior high school did not develop, grow, and achieve its present status because of any one of the enumerated factors; rather, it grew because of all of them. The credit for the junior high school cannot be given to Eliot, Thorndike, Hall, or any other individual. Nor can the growth of the junior high school be written off simply because reorganization provided administrators with an expediency solution to the schoolhouse shortage problem. Many were the individuals who contributed to the development of the junior high school and many were the conditions which supported its growth. It was the interaction of the many conditions and factors which caused the successful growth of the movement.

In some instances, even the champions of the junior high school movement came from different philosophical camps. College men advocated reorganization for economy of time. Public school leaders were concerned over better meeting immediate needs and saw the junior high school as a means of doing this. Board of education members may have seen reorganization as an economy move, while teachers may have supported reorganization because it would bring about new and improved special facilities such as science laboratories.

A dominant factor, however, has undergirded the successful development of the junior high school movement over the long haul. This has been the desire of educators to provide an appropriate educational program for early adolescents. Such a desire was both an original impetus and a continuing concern. While certainly not denying the assistance of other factors in the development of junior high school education, we may note that the support of some of these factors has not been sustained. For instance, the original reason for reorganization, economy of time, was the movement's first fatality. The dropout problem which motivated many early efforts to reorganize has largely been resolved at the junior high school level. The assistance which the junior high school received from the guidance movement is now given to other schools as well. But the attempt to provide an effective educational program based on the nature of young adolescents remains as the basic theme song of the junior high school movement.

Chronological coincidences

"Nine-tenths of wisdom," said Teddy Roosevelt, "is being wise in time." And while we cannot credit an institution such as the junior high school with wisdom, this statement may point up an important reason for the successful development of the American junior high school. Accidentally, coincidentally, and in some cases by design, the junior high school seems to have been wise in time. Its growth seems to have been assisted by many chronological coincidences. The way a variety of developments worked together to the advantage of the reorganization movement is at least a partial explanation for the notable success which the movement has enjoyed.

What if G. Stanley Hall had published his volumes on adolescence in 1925 instead of 1905? What if the schooling shortage caused by World War I had come before the series of committee reports dealing with reorganization rather than after? What if the dropout studies had been made in the 1880s rather than in 1907-1911? What if the movement to chart individual differences had come about before any mention of reorganization had been made? A number of similar questions might be posed, and probably would be equally difficult to answer with confidence. They are, perhaps, purely academic, yet they serve to point up how important the chronological convergence of numerous factors was to the growth and development of the junior high school.

In summary, many factors worked together to cause the inauguration and early success of the crusade to reorganize secondary education. The original impetus for reorganization came from the colleges and was concerned with economy of time and with college preparation. Discussions about reorganization then began to broaden their base. Proposals for reorganization became linked with other school problems, such as the high rate of elimination and retardation. From psychology came further justification. The culture provided fertile soil for the seeds of reorganization whether planted by college presidents, school administrators or by professional educators. So the movement to reorganize secondary education, coming at a propitious time, prospered.

The junior high school may not have been all that many hoped it would be. It may never have proved itself on some counts, yet it has achieved marked success in its relatively brief history. Many new educational practices and ideas have been tested in the junior high school. More experimentation is in the offing, as glimpses of the future are beginning to come into clearer focus. The junior high school story is then an unfinished one, but its success to date augurs well for the future. ▶

John H. Lounsbury

Assuring the Continued Success
of the Middle School

Published in *The Middle School: A Look Ahead*, Paul George (Ed.), NMSA, 1977

E ducation, like many other institutionalized activities, has a
tendency to go around in circles. What is past is, indeed,
prologue. The present sometimes turns out to be essentially
like the past. Progress can and often does come out of regression.
The movement to reorganize education which began circa 1910 has
been full circle. Much of what is happening in middle school
education today closely resembles earlier developments in junior
high school education as the cycle repeats itself. This may seem like
a note of despair or an expression of fatalism, but it is only intended to be a bit of realism and a point of perspective. History
does not always have to repeat itself.

The middle school must guard against becoming a victim of its
apparent success; pleased with its good press, its numerical status,
and its firm position aboard the bandwagon of the 70s. The more it
becomes institutionalized, the greater the danger of its becoming
petrified.

Even though the place of an intermediate institution in American
education is now fairly secure, its nature is still under discussion.
Securing a place in the education sun is not the primary task for the
middle school. In the language of the transescent, it needs to "hang
loose."

In the final analysis, the essence of the middle school movement
does not lie in the particular organization it advocates or its grade
level composition. Organizational distinctiveness is so readily
achievable that it is all too easy to let it become the only goal. The
essence of middle school education is, and ought to be, its philosophy of teaching and learning. Here is the major arena for implementing those fundamental questions of education that have
nagged thoughtful educators for many, many decades. It is, or ought

to be, a major manifestation of what was once called progressive education.

The middle school is not a new invention, and it ought not be mass produced as if it were an end in itself. Middle school education is, however, a means to an end. It is an exciting educational opportunity. The professional enthusiasm, commitment, and expertise that exist abundantly in the middle school movement should be exploited positively and fully. Our energies should focus on capitalizing on administrative reorganization and label switching for the purpose of working on instructional improvements; putting into practice more of what is known about teaching and learning. The locus of our major efforts in middle school education should be on the student-teacher relationship, for that is the only place in education where there is really a payoff.

The overuse of the class

The American educational system at the junior and senior high school levels has had only one major string on its organization-for-instruction violin; the string of a class, a group of 30 pupils assigned to a teacher for fifty minutes, with a responsibility to cover a particular body of knowledge. The vehicle of the class is the most overworked arrangement in education. Its excessive use is supported by long-standing tradition, widely held expectations, and administrative manageability, but not by research evidence on its efficacy. The middle school must institute alternatives, even if only to prove that the existing pattern does have value.

Somehow, some way, the middle school has to open up institutionalized education, to make possible professional diagnosis that is followed by professional prescription. Regrettably, the present structure not only makes individual diagnosis difficult, but most often all but pointless. It is hard to escape the conclusion that schools generally have been either unable or unwilling to provide an education that is truly fitted to individual beings.

The traditional schedule, and its counterpart of the graded system, is convenient and acceptable in a system that, while it wouldn't want to admit it, is heavily committed to providing custodial care. In such a system it seems to make sense to catalog youngsters, label them, and treat them as members of some group. The educator's role often becomes heavily weighted toward that of a caretaker, concerned with bells and schedules, lockers and ledgers. Multiage grouping in athletics and band is readily accepted, but the academic program is held in lockstep.

We start out in the middle school with the greatest diversity that exists in the twelve grades of public education, and then we organize a school which is in direct conflict with this diversity. We organize kids into herds, based on chronological age and call them grades, then divide them into pens based on an arbitrary number and supposed likeness in one trait and call them classes. We then move groups through an all too common curriculum. Indeed, at this level when young people exhibit greatest diversity, we often present them a more standardized and common program than any other time in the educational process.

About the nature and needs of early adolescents there is no mystery. They are very open, making their thoughts and behaviors very evident, and "playing games" far less often than adults. They are normal. Sometimes we have even over-emphasized their distinctiveness and uniqueness, for on careful analysis no completely new traits appear during this period; none occur solely at this level. We are dealing with rapidly developing and expanding characteristics rather than unique ones. Too, so much of what is difficult or distinctive about early adolescence is culturally caused rather than innate.

Whether or not we adequately provide for the needs of middle school youngsters, we know they are growing physically, and need lots of exercise, some competition, but also some rest and quiet. They have intellectual prowess and need challenge rather than just repetition and drill. They need discussion, the opportunity to experiment, to sample, They are filled with emotions that lie close to the surface. They still need structure, but they also need opportunities for free expression in literature, poetry and art. They are, of course, highly conscious of their peers and their opinions.

The Herculean task of providing education for all American youth has inevitably resulted in a reliance on organizing a system built to accommodate masses. It was easy to slip into the pattern of the simple self-contained classroom at the elementary school level and the teacher-class-subject arrangement at the secondary level. Soon a general pattern emerged that became standard for secondary education. It could be expressed as a formula: Ed. = 30x6x5x36. If there was anything to be taught, fit it into the formula. Get thirty students, offer a class in one of six periods for five days a week and continue for thirty-six weeks. Sometimes slight alterations, such as eighteen weeks or thirty-five pupils were accepted, but by and large the one basic formula was and still is followed. The junior high school soon fell into this secondary pattern despite considerable experimentation with the core curriculum. Likewise there is danger that the intermediate unit, now usually called the middle school, will fall victim to the tradition and administrative simplicity of the subject-class arrangement.

The key to continued success

The middle school movement will be a continuing success to the degree that it is able to break with the departmentalized, subject-centered curriculum that has been an albatross around the neck of intermediate education for decades. So long as our pattern of organization perpetuates the notion that all youngsters in the same class should learn the same material at the same time in the same way, the middle school will fail to achieve its goals. Groups, grades, and classes are administrative arrangements far more than they are appropriate instructional strategies for transescent youth. A class doesn't learn, it has no mind. A grade has little commonality other than a general chronological age, and groups are never really homogeneous. A teacher's lesson, no matter how well thought out and professionally presented, is seldom right for an entire class. The teacher-class system has led to a situation wherein teachers are so busy teaching "classes" that they don't have time to direct the education of youth. Procedures need to be developed that support the total development of individuals as well as supporting the acquisition of information. Means must be found to give affective education a firm place in the middle school.

America's middle school is still on the cutting edge. It has engendered much excitement, broad involvement, and considerable experimentation. It must now avoid the easy temptation to standardize, becoming set and satisfied with grade level reorganization and a new label. Continued success depends upon continuing efforts to break the lock step of the teacher-subject-class arrangement.

Let all of us who have a real interest in the education of transescents make the most of the tremendous opportunity which the middle school movement presents. Let us keep our eyes on the diverse youth we serve. Let their needs take precedence over teachers' preferences based on obsolete subject-centered preparation programs. Let us have the courage of our deep convictions, willing to break with the safe, standard teacher-class-subject arrangement. For only as we turn classrooms into laboratories and convert teachers from "tellers" to directors of learning will the separate middle grade educational unit be justified and effective. ◗

John H. Lounsbury reflects...

What is Past is Prologue

Experienced politicians long ago discovered that statements made years before under different circumstances can come back to haunt you. In times of rapid change such as those occurring in the last forty some years, opinions expressed in one decade often seem awfully dated and off-base when reread in the present.

So it was with some trepidation that I went back to review my earliest writing on the junior high school, before the term middle school had been advanced. But to my surprise – and admitted delight – the views expressed were ones I could still stand by.

The first article I published forty-two years ago advanced the notion that a new model of the junior high school was in the offing as this uniquely American institution underwent a renaissance. Some descriptors of things to come in this new model included such comments as these:

> *The modern model does not fly the banner of departmentalization.*

> *The proponents of ability grouping are not nearly so numerous among the goodly company (of the new junior high school).*

Rereading that 1956 piece with its optimistic call for a renaissance and a reformation of the junior high school led me to conclude that I really was correct. Such a reformation has occurred, for the new model of the junior high school *is* the middle school.

The obstacles that kept junior from growing up that were cited in the 1960 *Clearing House* article are still present today and continue to hinder the middle school's development. The one exception is the barrier of an unfortunate label. The name problem has largely been obliterated by the recent wide acceptance of the terms *middle school* and *middle level education* in both the professional and public press. Regrettably, the lack of distinctive teacher education and certification in most states continues as a barrier.

In the relatively recent (1977) article, the first I wrote that dealt exclusively with the middle school rather than the junior high school, I called for an end to departmentalization. To ensure its continued success, I stated, the middle school had to break with the departmentalized, subject-centered curriculum. The article is fully contemporary in 1998 – twenty-one years later. The only thing that dates it is the use of the term *transescent*.

Rereading these articles makes it apparent that progress in reforming education has been painfully slow – even for middle level education which has been in the vanguard of school improvement efforts since the 1960s. Although there has been a great deal of discussion about "innovations," on careful analysis there aren't many truly new educational ideas. In many fundamental ways, the current middle school movement is simply the rebirth of progressive education. Although some of the terminology has changed (interdisciplinary planning rather than correlation, or student involvement rather than student-teacher planning, or integrated learning rather than problem-centered learning), the advocacies advanced today are little different from those of several decades ago.

Having looked back, looked around, and reflected a bit, it is inevitable that I would look ahead and was requested to do so by the editor. And having just noted the disappointingly little progress that has occurred either in the ideas proposed or the practices utilized, one might expect a rather dire prediction for the near future. Should we expect the slow pace of educational reform witnessed over nearly a century to continue at this snail's pace? Will the recent advocacy of middle level educators prove to continue more as rhetoric than reality?

I've often been accused of being a naïve optimist, and not without good cause, so I will remain true to form and offer a scenario of major changes in the next twenty-two years, changes far, far greater than have occurred in the last seventy-five years. (It is not likely that I'll have to face these predictions, so why not dream optimistically?)

The middle school of 2020 exists today in many places and pieces. While no one school as yet has all the elements in operation, there are schools successfully practicing all of the features that will become accepted characteristics in good middle level schools of 2020. It is not necessary to "invent" new educational practices. It is not even essential to conduct some wholly new research study to secure evidence now lacking, for the research supporting the middle school concept is now accumulating.

I fervently hope, and expect, that after two decades of the new century we will no longer be restricted in our thinking about the formal educational process by the terms *courses, subjects, grades,* and *periods.* Currently, educators and others seem unable to discuss schooling practices without assuming the continued use of the above vehicles and terms. They may advocate newer courses – but still courses. They believe we should connect the subjects – but they still assume subjects will exist as entities. They discuss adding, subtracting, or combining periods in the schedule – but still assume schools will have periods and classes. To reform education as it needs to be we must be able to think above and beyond those restrictive terms that limit the possibilities.

In a recent story advancing the idea of the year-round school, the author claimed that under this arrangement the "curriculum would be delivered more efficiently," and further that the year-round school would be "delivering an education in an efficient year-round package." In my view the curriculum is not something to be "delivered," nor can an education be "packaged." Putting to rest such invalid and narrow assumptions about what constitutes an education will be a major task in the near future. Until these limited understandings about the curriculum can be corrected, the fundamental changes in the schooling process that are needed will be nearly impossible to achieve.

Someway, somehow we must help the public grasp a bigger and better vision of what is involved in an "education." The public and much of the profession are handicapped by a narrow vision built on false assumptions about learning and teaching. The needed reforms in education will not be achieved by more dollars, more programs, improved facilities, or by "restructuring," desirable as all of those things may be. To really reform education we must alter people's attitudes and understandings about what constitutes an education, throw light on the largely false assumptions that underlie the traditional processes of schooling, and enlarge their vision of schooling. The whole age-grade structure, for example, is not supported by what we now know about human growth and development, yet it continues to enjoy the unquestioned status of an eternal verity. And teaching still is conceived to be largely a matter of telling, and learning is thought to be a matter of assimilating and retaining information.

But believing that – if you'll excuse the use of an old cliché – "the middle school is an idea whose time has come," and that we will, indeed, make that paradigm shift so often talked about. I see good middle level schools in the year 2020 characterized by such conditions as these:

1. There will be no uniform schedule of periods, no master schedule that looks like a day's program in *TV Guide*. No bells, no mass changing of classes at regular intervals. New schools will not feature rectangular classrooms opening into a common hallway.
2. There will be no single subject-graded textbooks issued to each pupil and presumed to encompass what is to be taught.
3. Teams will consist of two or three rather than four or five teachers.
4. Multiage teams and student-teacher progression plans, while still not universal, will be common.
5. Advisory programs, as separate entities, will have disappeared in the more advanced middle schools as truly integrated learning will readily encompass the affective, students' socio-psychological concerns, and related matters. The pastoral role of all middle level teachers will be recognized and honored.
6. There will be no computer labs as computers and other forms of technology effective in promoting learning will be available in the flexible learning centers where students will have individual learning stations.

7. Grading periods of six or nine weeks culminating in the school-wide distribution of letter grade report cards will no longer exist. The assessment of student progress will be ongoing, student-centered, authentic, and largely non-competitive. Assessment activities will focus on acquiring desirable behavioral attributes as much as on acquiring discrete knowledge and skills, and all learnings will be documented in students' structured portfolios.

8. Students will not remain captive in their isolated school facilities but rather they will frequently engage in learning and service activities away from the school in community sites.

9. Parents and other family members will be more accepting of their important roles and will be actively engaged in the youngster's school progress. Communities likewise will be closely aligned with their schools.

10. Helping pupils develop their personal set of values will be an acknowledged responsibility of the school. The traditional task of citizenship education will be broadened and more directly confronted.

Perhaps more than 22 years will be needed to make such changes common in all middle level schools. But, I believe, there are good reasons for feeling positive about the years ahead and the changes that are in the offing. The following conditions justify my optimism.

1. **The existence of the National Middle School Association as a viable professional organization that has clout.** The junior high school of the 20s, 30s, and 40s had no such national organization and voice. In addition to NMSA itself there are now more than fifty state, regional, provincial, and international affiliates of NMSA with combined membership of hundreds of thousands. The newsletters, conferences, publications, and other activities of these associations touch these thousands regularly and will continue to exert a positive influence. Several other major professional organizations are also promoting middle level education.

2. **The growing dissatisfaction with the state of America's public schools and the awareness that our high school graduates are not well prepared for life in the 21st century.** No one, it seems, wants the status quo to continue. The federal government, state governments, foundations, parent organizations, business leaders, and others are all calling for reform. Change, then, is going to come.

3. **The increasingly acknowledged critical state of our society characterized by rampant violence, crime, drug abuse, teenage pregnancy, and other sordid conditions that make it clear we must change the attitudes and behavior of our youth.** And who can change that behavior? Where can it occur? The answers are middle level teachers in middle level schools. The public is gradually coming to recognize that the experiences youth undergo as they move through the years from 10 to 15 have lifelong influence. And given the diminished influence of families, neighborhoods, communities, and even religious institutions, the roles of the school and its teachers in building both character and academic competence become paramount.

4. **The advancement of our knowledge base relative to the period of early adolescence and the research findings regarding effective educational practices at the middle level.** The junior high school had no such foundation in human development and educational research. While most adults still lack an adequate appreciation of the significance of the years from 10 to 15 that lack is under attack and is gradually being replaced with needed understandings on the part of parents concerning "coming of age." Activities such as The Month of the Young Adolescent are succeeding in their educational mission. Research on the middle school concept, while still in its infancy, now has a vigorous life, and it will continue to advance. And certainly the new advocacy for implementing middle school practices at the high school level bodes well for the future. A greatly expanding body of professional literature is now available for study by educators and parents alike.

5. Finally – and foremost – my optimism is fueled by what I have witnessed and felt in middle level schools all across America and beyond. **Middle level classroom teachers by the hundreds are doing good things for kids.** The middle school movement has given teachers and principals the opportunity and the encouragement to break the mold, to follow their hearts rather than tradition, to practice their real philosophies rather than continuing to "keep school." Although coming from both elementary and high school backgrounds both lacking in middle level pre-service education, these courageous teachers have implemented newer and more effective practices, ones that have led to improved student achievement and personal development. If one wants to see cutting edge practices, increased student involvement, teachers as collegial professionals, go to a middle school. There you will find genuinely committed teachers who do care about student achievement but also much, much more. Despite the skepticism of many adults who evidence little appreciation and often overt opposition, good teachers are doing good things for kids in hundreds of our middle schools. They are giving life to a movement that is based on our best understandings of the learning process and the nature of young adolescents. With such foundations the middle school concept will continue to thrive and ultimately gain the victory. ◗

IV

Conrad F. Toepfer, Jr.

The articles I selected dealt with middle level issues I saw as important at the time of writing. While conditions have changed, these issues continue to have significance for middle level education. The first one dealt with the perennial problem of teacher education. Published in 1965, it makes it clear how slow progress has been. The second article identified central issues in early efforts to define a middle school curricular rationale – a need that persists. ASCD was the first national organization to devote major emphasis to middle level education concerns, and the third article appeared in the first major publication developed by ASCD's Council on Emerging Adolescent Learners. It identified central and largely unresolved middle level educational issues. The last and more recent article was developed from my general session address to the second NMSA Annual Conference (1975). The characteristics identified in it remain helpful, I believe, in developing middle level school programs that respond effectively to young adolescent developmental/learning needs.

CONRAD F. TOEPFER, JR.

Who Should Teach in Junior High?

Published in *The Clearing House*, October, 1965

General opinion assumes that the junior high school evolved in an attempt to meet the educational needs of early adolescence. In reality, though, the junior high school has evolved, for the most part, because of almost every other conceivable need. The past decade, however has seen a greater focus upon organizing the junior high school in terms of the needs of the early adolescent student. While such attempts have been spasmodic and "topsy-like" in growth, American public education is coming to the realization that the early adolescent junior high school student is distinctly different, not only from the elementary school student, as recognized for decades, but from the senior high school student as well. If this is true, teacher education should provide the junior high school teacher with a preparation distinctly different from preparation to teach in elementary or senior high school. Overwhelmingly, this is not the case today. The junior high school has steadily become part and parcel of the American public school system and appears to be here to stay. Who should teach in the junior high school? The answer is obvious: junior high school teachers! What should the education of the junior high school teacher be? This answer, unfortunately, is not so readily available.

The junior high school teacher is fish as well as fowl. Most states provide an overlapping certification which allows the candidate to teach in the elementary grades as well as in the junior high grades. Certification to teach in the junior high school is usually granted the elementary school teacher upon his completion of some specific subject matter specialization above his basic elementary certification requirements. At the same time, most states similarly structure the certification of secondary school teachers to be inclusive of the early secondary or junior high school grades as well. In few such instances are there any specific or additional requirements for certification to teach in the junior high school. Thus, the area of junior high school teacher education and certification is "no man's land." There is a tragically myopic lack of definition of the experiences needed by teachers working with the early adolescent students which the junior high school typically serves.

Some of the lack of success of the American secondary school may well stem from the beginnings of frustration developed in the junior high school. Certainly the lack of teachers specifically educated to work with a student as unique as the early adolescent junior high school student may be a strong contributing factor toward developing an educational climate in which student frustrations are germinated. Junior high school teachers commonly fail to understand the problems of early adolescence and the extremely personal nature of the difficulties typically faced by an individual in approaching, achieving, and adjusting to adolescence. Similarly, they often do not understand the causes for the erratic behavior of many early adolescent students and their relatively short attention and interest spans.

The organization of curriculum and instruction in the junior high school might be significantly different from what it is, were it to be based upon a sufficiently broad and deep knowledge of the early adolescent student. Within this setting of frustration and lack of understanding, problems of student morale and holding power may well be conceived for development in the senior high school. These differences have important ramifications for the areas of teaching methodology and technique, curriculum planning, and, above all, consideration for the psychological development of students. Teacher education for elementary and senior high school certification has been built upon the recognized important needs of both areas. If, however, as appears to be the growing trend, it can be agreed that the student in the junior high school is significantly different from both the elementary and the senior high school student, these differences should be translatable into a program of education not only for junior high school students but for junior high school teachers. The implications of this are two-pronged for undergraduate as well as graduate teacher education.

The University of Indiana at Bloomington has pioneered a program in junior high school teacher education and certification for almost three years. Dr. John E. Reisert developed the Indiana program in a sincere attempt to organize a teacher education experience based upon important needs of teachers at the junior high school level. The program, however, has had considerably less than monumental success, with few students having elected this sequence. This is attributable to the fact that teachers in Indiana may still qualify for a secondary certificate allowing them to teach in grades 7 through 12. The Indiana experience indicates that the development of a program of education for junior high school teachers without the support of certification requirements will, in all probability, prove to be a noble but relatively ineffective experiment. Not only must teacher education define and develop specific experiences and requirements for the education and certification of junior high school teachers, but the back door entrance for either elementary or secondary teachers to function at the junior high school level with a "catch-as-catch-can" preparation must be sealed off.

No matter what educational innovations may be developed to meet the needs of the junior high school student and regardless of the degree to which such changes may be implemented, the success of such attempts will be less than we should like until we develop and implement a succinct educational experience for junior high school teachers. If the junior high school student is unique, his teachers must be educated in programs distinctly different from those for prospective elementary and senior high school teachers. Awareness of the important differences in the natures of the preadolescent, adolescent, and later adolescent student served by the junior high school must be learned by junior high school teachers. They must then be prepared to organize instruction in terms of the educational needs of their students. They must also be educated to understand the importance of exploration in planning curricula and organizing instruction in the junior high school. Their techniques of instruction should also differ from those at the elementary or senior high school level.

Programs of undergraduate teacher education for junior high school teachers should carefully identify the age group in which the prospective candidate has the most interest and with which he may have better skills in terms of communication as it would affect his teaching. Opportunities to observe the differences between elementary and junior high school situations, on the one hand, and junior high and senior high school situations, on the other, should be provided so that the decision as to the level at which prospective teachers wish to specialize can be made upon a solid basis of understanding. The curricula of teacher education programs and their observation, participation, and student teaching experiences should then be directed specifically toward the appropriate level.

Graduate teacher education programs should also be organized for the special needs of the junior high school teacher. These graduate experiences must be supported by state certification requirements to add the kind of emphasis currently built into graduate experiences for elementary and senior high school teachers. Such experiences should include study of the psychology of early adolescence, teaching methods, and organization of junior high school instruction, as well as careful consideration of the role and objectives of the junior high school in the total scope of elementary and secondary education.

The junior high school has been and will be expected to achieve specific objectives in the education of students as they progress through the American public school system. The lack of definition of the education suitable for the junior high school teacher, as compared with the elementary and senior high teacher, would seem to indicate that the prospects for success of teachers in junior high schools must be considerably less than at the other two levels. This is not to imply that the junior high school has not achieved some distinct successes or that it has not been a positive movement in the development of the American public school system. It is of paramount importance that American education is realizing there are distinct differences between junior high school students and both elementary and senior high school students. However, this now must be followed by the identification of an experience in teacher education which will allow the junior high school teacher to develop greater perceptions and understandings of his task. The junior high school teacher might then really be educated to operate with the realistic awareness and skills needed to achieve the objectives which the junior high school has fervently sought for well over half a century. ▶

Reprinted with permission of the Helen Dwight Reid Educational Foundation. Published by Heldref Publications, 1319 Eighteenth St., N.W., Washington, D.C. 20036-1802. Copyright © 1965 *The Clearing House* (V. 40, October, 1965, pp. 74-76).

Curricular Imperatives for the Middle School

Published in *The Quarterly,* ASCD, April, 1969

T he saga of American public school organization since 1900 has been a kaleidoscope of changing forms and patterns. Its evolving milieu has been replete with rapid changes in vogue, fads, and bandwagons, unfortunately not always well-thought-out as planned improvement upon existent situations. To be fair, one must recognize the demands or pressures which caused many such trial and error episodes. However, it is hoped that future change in school organization will become a more stabilized evolution based upon thoughtful and systematic improvement of the educational enterprise.

A specific look et early secondary education during the last three decades tempts one to view it as akin to a "soap opera" serial, replete with a due succession of heroes, villains, and a "constant cavalcade of cliffhanging crises!" Now a new hero enters the scene to try and save the early adolescent from lost identity, "Mighty Middle School!" As the newcomer moves to center-stage this new episode faces the old familiar questions. "Will the characteristics of the adolescent ever be prime determinants of the pattern for his education?" "Will schools for early adolescents ever be organized upon a curricular rather an administrative rationale?"

No disparagement of the middle school concept is intended here. As an educational innovation enjoying the initial glory of the "Hawthorne effect," it is getting the full red carpet treatment accorded most new organizational approaches, including a share of professional literature and hasty (although sometimes short-lived) adoption by increasing numbers of school systems. It is not hard to find some school systems that made an early move to middle school organization now moving back to older patterns. Such unfortunate experiences have doubtless left a definite disillusionment with embryonic educational innovations. Properly, however, this should be recognized as moving too rapidly from an established pattern without (1) identifying what the new pattern can do better than the present one; and (2) developing a planned approach for systematically moving to the pattern if the existing pattern seems irrevocably effective.

The middle school concept can be a significant improvement in early secondary education if it is defined in terms of the characteristics of early adolescents and then systematically planned to actualize proved learning experiences for them. A logical approach would seem to be: (1) identify and study nature, characteristics and educational needs of early adolescents as a learner group; (2) develop a curricular rationale which will best compliment those needs in a school setting; and (2) organize an administrative vehicle to expedite such a program. Failure of previous early secondary school patterns to so order their own development has raised considerable apprehension that the middle school concept may be just another administrative whim to which early adolescent learners will be subjected. Regrettably it is not difficult to find junior high school administrators who conclude that all that needs be done to achieve the unfulfilled objectives of the junior high school is to replace it with a middle school organization, add water, and stir. The only predictable result of such a nostrum would seem to be a continued lack of definitive curricular programs for early adolescents!

A modicum of this was personally observed visiting a midwestern community last summer. Upon hearing that the local school system was moving to a middle school organization, a visit was paid to the junior high school making the transition. In a meeting with the school principal, questions were asked as to what changes would be made for the coming fall. In all seriousness came the reply that the sign on the school building and the school stationery would be changed to middle school but that nothing else was contemplated for a year or so. The principal emphasized that "the middle school was the next big thing in the field and that we want to be certain that we're on the ground floor." In answer to questions about reorganizing the balance of grades in the system's elementary and secondary buildings, program changes, etc., the reply was that "only time would tell whether or not it was really worth going to all that trouble." Yet this school system is presently listed in a bibliography of a major educational organization among those that have "moved to a middle school organization!"

This legacy of reshuffling of form has not given adequate consideration to the specific educational substance of early secondary education. Such changes have been based largely upon administrative expedience with minimal curricular reorganization for instructional improvement. As a result, the clientele of early adolescent learners in early secondary schools probably has experienced less discrete definition of basic curricular experiences than those at either the elementary or high school level. This definition should become a primary operational task of the middle school concept. The imperative nature of this need dictates that in order to develop integrity, the middle school concept must closely define and specify its projected effectiveness over existing patterns in early secondary education.

It is the junior high school as the dominant pattern in early secondary education which the middle school is challenging. It is not advocated here that the junior high school establishment be overthrown without analyzing whether or not it can be reorganized as an effective educational pattern for early adolescents. Careful specification of its objectives and functions might reveal the junior high school to have strong potential as a superior pattern for early secondary education. This possibility should be investigated before arbitrarily deciding to follow the middle school parade. However, history does not reveal that the junior high school has been particularly based upon early adolescent learner needs. Study of school board minutes and other primary sources in communities where the junior high school originated and grew indicates that expediencies were the prime causes for the development of that pattern of school organization (Toepfer, 1962). One cannot obviate the reality of local conditions and their supportive rationale for school organization, but as the prime or sole motives for reorganizing the educational environment of learners they only corrupt the purposes of education. It is a fact that despite the passing of fifty-some years since origin, the junior high school has not yet organized a succinct and agreed-upon curricular rationale to support its administrative evolution. Even in its inception the junior high school did not validate its projected improvement over the effectiveness of the existing school patterns which it sought to replace. In admonishing the halo effect which the early junior high school movement was gaining, Thomas Kirby (1927) made this keen observation:

> Changes in our American schools are frequent. Our assumption is that the change is an improvement but there are few instances where the condition before the change or after it was carefully enough evaluated so that progress or regression could be claimed with assurance. The Junior High School has been accepted with such alacrity that about two-thirds of the cities in the United States of 100,000 population have adopted it or are moving in that direction. To what extent is this new organization an improvement over that which it displaced or is displacing? Do results show that the enthusiastic supporters of this movement are justified in the extravagant claims which they have made? It is time to begin taking stock while there still remains enough of the old organization to set the new. (p. 3)

Evaluation of any institution's effectiveness should seek to identify how successfully it has achieved its own stated purposes and objectives. To this end, the continued failure of the junior high school to develop a curricular rationale has rendered even contemporary assessment of its effectiveness most difficult. Unfortunately, such lack of definition by middle school concept in its own short history would appear to make it vulnerable to a similar fate. Likewise, the plethora of writing emerging about middle schools reflects only minor concern with trying to establish a curricular basis.

It is submitted, then, that the immediate task confronting the middle school concept is the development of a succinct curricular rationale as an operational model. Such a statement must identify how middle school will be organized upon the identified character-istics of early adolescents and how this will improve upon what previous patterns have achieved. This would require careful defini-tion of the substance of the educative experience in early secondary education, something virtually overlooked in its long-standing infatuation with form. It may well be that much of improving the effectiveness of early secondary education has to do with making organizational form more compatible with its educational essence. Not having yet undertaken this study, for all we know the relation between form and substance in existing early secondary school programs may be as effective as hot soup in brown paper bags! Such a program of self-definition is an ambitious task for the middle school and will require a procedural development. The following considerations are recommended in formulating these procedures.

The definition of a curricular rationale by the middle school will require identification of the contemporary characteristics of adoles-cents as a learner group. This information should be a foundation for realistic explication of learner needs at this level and serve as a basis for organizing patterns of instruction within the middle school. These data can then be organized as a curriculum design and stated as specific educational objectives of the middle school. This information should suggest new directions for reorganizing other units of the school system. By "other units of the school system" it is intended that both the elementary and the high school could study their organization in terms of this evidence.

The lowering of the age of pubescence during the past half century in America has ramifications for elementary as well as early secondary education. If grade six or grades five and six are placed in the middle school, then this shortened scope of elementary education along with earlier pre-pubescent maturation may provide reasons for rethinking elementary school organization. Likewise, the reallocation of grade nine to the school should require broad reorganization of the school as a four-year unit. Carried to its logical conclusion, the extension of this study into the elementary and high schools could lead to a K-12 curricular rationale, something not new to the theory and practice of system-wide curriculum planning. Of immediate concern to the issue at hand, however, is that the lack of such definition in early secondary education meant that unmet educational needs of early adolescents today furnish a most critical point of undertaking such study. This is the gauntlet which the middle school must pick up.

Completion of this Herculean task by the middle school would place it in an enviable position. It could then develop a rationale for choosing organizational facets designed to achieve its stated objectives. The range of these facets, of scheduling, special and supportive services, etc., all could then be selected and planned in terms of stated objectives to compliment early adolescent learner characteristics. As tardy as this may be, it would be the first time that this evidence has been gathered and utilized as the basis for making such decisions.

If the middle school concept is to succeed where previous patterns of early secondary education failed, it must take a thrust which will cause it to become involved with these curricular imperatives. From this beachhead, the long elusive objective of "articulation of the school system" may be attainable. ▶

References

Kirby, T. (1927). *Preface to an evaluation of special purposes of junior high school: Economy of time and bridging the gap.* Iowa City: IA. Ralph A. Fritz, University of Iowa Studies, Vol. IV, No. 5.

Toepfer, C.F., Jr. (1962). Evolving curricular patterns in junior high schools. . . An historical study. Unpublished doctoral dissertation, State University of New York, Buffalo.

Some Operational Problems in Educating Emerging Adolescent Learners

Published in *Educational Dimensions of the Early Adolescent Learner*, N. Atkins & P. Pumcrantz (Eds.), ASCD, 1973

Although pubescent development is universal, the unpredictably early or late arrival at adolescent capability makes this period of human growth a frustrating and traumatic one. As the individual contemplates his personal progress in approaching adolescence, his anticipations are both frightening and exciting; and his achievement of these tasks in mind, body, and psyche remain eternally personal.

The operational problems encountered in attempts of the American public school to educate its emerging adolescent learner population are both inherited and created. In the instance of inherited problems, both the relative inflexibility and insensitivity of school organization as regards societal changes and the isolation of planning of the educative institution from the total societal-communal spectrum have combined to create a communication gap between theory and reality. As to created problems, the history of the junior high school and in many instances the evolving middle school movement both give dismaying evidence of perpetuating the syndrome of inherited problems by failure to define objectives and functions in terms of the dynamic needs and capabilities of the emerging adolescent. The academic evolution of method, content, material, and activities at this level continues to be cloudy and nebulous – and for the most part similar to the general academic orientation of secondary education. This persists because the role and function of the educative experience for emerging adolescents have not been determined in terms of identifiable needs at this developmental level.

Operationally, these problems seem to lie in four progressive stages which reflect both the learner's needs in emerging adolescence and society's need to provide for his transition in achieving his own human self-definition. These are (1) exploring individual interests and needs; (2) developing a realistic and positive self-concept; (3) developing individual social, intellectual, and living skills; and, (4) formulating possible future roles in ensuing school, occupational, and societal settings.

Exploring individual interests and needs

While schools for emerging adolescents have long offered exploratory courses in their curriculum sequences, these experiences have almost inevitably been better in thought than in deed. One semester of academic offerings in areas such as art, music, industrial arts, homemaking, foreign languages, and business subjects has long endured in the departmentalized program in the seventh and eighth grades. The sad fact has been that these programs have been content-oriented, graded, and averaged in with the student's total achievement for purposes of pupil reporting, permanent records, honor rolls, etc. The result has been that students have approached these courses viewing them as part of the total academic regimen of the school. The courses of study in these "exploratory" offerings have been teacher- or State Department of Instruction-prescribed, and at best, punitive. Only those students who happen to like and/or do well in these areas through coincidence of their interests and the prescribed program can gain a positive experience.

The degree to which even these experiences are at all exploratory is virtually negligible. Schools serving emerging adolescents have yet to organize programs which will take a "broach" approach to exploration in all areas of interest and study. Pupil-teacher planning of such experiences in terms of focus and content is essential if student needs are to be accommodated. The question of individual readiness for different kinds of exploratory experiences must be carefully considered for each specific experience. In some cases a specific experience should be deferred to a later time or repeated if a readiness develops that was not present in the initial exposure. Approaches to evaluation must obviate the concept of failure in this setting. The identification by the student and his teacher that he is doing well, is not interested in or ready for a specific situation should be in itself a critical success in the student's self-exploration.

The need for a careful interrelation of the instructional and pupil personnel staff is paramount to the development of such an approach to exploration.

Developing a realistic, positive self-concept

National mental health sources indicate that after accidental death, suicide is the second leading cause of emerging adolescent mortality. Likewise, the rate of increase of suicide and attempted suicide is higher in this group than any other. This combined with apathy and rejection reflected in our adolescent and post-adolescent society points to the need for the development of a realistic, positive, self-concept by our youth. This characteristic is observable in a great majority of students leaving elementary school. However, in the years of emerging adolescence this capacity seems to falter. Thus, the middle school must plan its total program to help its students develop this perspective as they approach and achieve adolescence. The student at this level needs to know and understand his personal intellectual, physical, and emotional strengths and weaknesses. Middle school programs must help him to accept these realities and make an effective adjustment to what he is and what he may become. Education during this period should help him explore ways of building a bridge into his approaching future and develop skills as his profile of needs requires. In the main, schools for emerging adolescents have procrastinated, prevaricated, and obviated this responsibility for the great mass of students. Only those students fortunate to have adequate or above average "luck-of-the-draw" in intellectual, physical, social, and emotional maturity have had realistic success.

Developing individual social, intellectual, and living skills

The third of these operational problems grows from recognition of the need to develop a continuing self-exploration and a realistic, positive self-concept. This should help focus the identification and development of basic social, intellectual, and living skills which the emerging adolescent needs to acquire. The school today can predict many of the demands of society at-large, as well as occupational and academic requirements for entrance and advancement both in the world of work and further study. More immediately, we know the necessity for a range of skills to understand and assimilate content, advanced skills, and other aspects of learning which high school and other educational situations shall demand. The organization of learning experiences around these areas of skill then should supplant a content emphasis in middle schools. With these skills (hopefully their development from the motivation of an improved, realistic, and positive self-concept) the emerging adolescent himself will more effectively be able to learn content and information with a greater personal awareness of his objectives as a learner.

Formulating possible future roles in ensuing school, occupational, and societal settings

The problem areas cited here, specifically this final one, cannot be totally overcome within the framework of the educational unit serving emerging adolescents. Anything approaching satisfactory amelioration of present problems will require an articulated and coordinated planning of the total K-12 educational spectrum. We can see too many situations in which sincere and competent attempts to improve education for a local emerging adolescent population have suffered because the high school program is not designed to build a continuum from the middle unit. In these tragic instances, the middle unit has provided students with skills, readiness, and enthusiasm which the high school dooms to frustration and disillusionment in its ossified, subject-centered, teacher-dominated totality. A continuing exploratory focus must be actualized in the high school for evolving self-concept and the learner's skill development. This means that academic, social, and possibly pre-vocational aspects of the curriculum in the high school must be offered in a setting where a comprehensive education program can emerge through the dynamics of pupil-teacher planning. Those tentative choices and initial directions which the emerging adolescent establishes in the middle unit of the system must be available or within the range of the high school experience. Because this seldom exists today, the learner cannot clarify and solidify possible academic, occupational, or social directions or establish new ones if initial experiences in those directions are not what was desired. As far from existing practice as this continuum is for the vast majority of emerging students who are jammed into our predestined pigeon holes of the junior high or middle school and high school amalgamation, this disestablishment of present practices must be achieved.

In summary to these four points, the challenge to overcome these unmet problems in educating our emerging adolescents must focus upon individualizing their education. The unique profiles of preadolescents become even more diffused in this emerging adolescent stage. The assembly line posture of schools for this middle level cannot accommodate the human needs which students bring to it. Despite the unique abilities, disabilities, and individual developmental patterns which children bring to the situation of the middle unit in our school system, each child is run through the educational machine regardless of his own readiness and is exposed to the predestined organization which the machine has scheduled to dispense. It is hoped that a significant percentage of students (that blessed group known as "our average developers") are within shooting distance of readiness when specific educational experiences have been implemented. However, we cannot state with certainty how many children with unique developmental precocity or tardiness have been swept aside, confounded, or irreparably damaged by the middle unit's singleness of form and inflexible, insensitive organization. We might wish, however, that as with "Barbarella," the unique person would break the machine instead of the reverse! These daily tragedies require that we gear education for emerging adolescents to compliment and satisfy these needs rather than subvert or smash them as presently occurs.

These four general problem areas will require considerable specification before remediation can be calculated. The following may provide a frame of reference for such specification.

1. Physical development and growth - universal yet idiosyn - cratic attainment of physical maturity.

> Puberty - female 10-13; male, 12-15
> Growth spurts

Sex differences within sexes

Psychological implications of physical and psychological differences

2. Status seeking - emancipations, vocational interests.

Emancipation from home provides the greatest barrier because home has provided the greatest security

An irregular but definite movement from dependence of childhood to independence expected of an adult

3. Major importance of peer group relations, homosexual and heterosexual.

Emancipation (from point 2) is aided by peer group and impeded by resurgence of Oedipal impulses – end of latency and confusion about male-female roles

4. Development and reevaluation of values with increasing awareness of self.

Development and reevaluation of values with special emphasison awareness of self, especially physical self

5. Time of intellectual expansion, academic experience, asceticism.

Intellectual expansion: academic experience and asceticism come into play in later adolescence in conjunction with:

1. Increased acceptance of new physical capacities

2. Increased emancipation

3. Increased vocational and status seeking

May be emphasized in later adolescence when most pupils have at least achieved puberty and social values (adult fees)

Intellectual expansion is also a defense – a means of self-protection

The middle unit of the school system is supposed to serve in a transitional capacity in order to serve the new and changing needs of the emerging adolescent. Yet, where has it solved existing operational problems by accommodating the following interests of the emerging adolescent?

1. sex
2. age
3. intelligence
4. socioeconomic status
5. residence
6. physical endowment
7. opportunities
8. period in history

What about the role of heterosexual relationships? The junior high school has purported to meet such needs.

1. Supposedly preparing students for high school
   a. by watering down high school activities
   b. not by defining and creating activities primarily suited to the developmental needs of the young adolescent, e.g., gym for girls.

2. Not taking advantage of capabilities of early adolescence
   a. homosexual activities, especially gangs still predominate at this age – why force heterosexual activities?
   b. fantasy activities great here to help in sex and social adjustment, where is this utilized in English literature classes?
   c. role playing – how have junior high schools helped young adolescents find identities of their own-to help them make beginnings toward such self-definition?

The middle unit has not developed an educational program designed to meet the needs of the young adolescent. It had adapted all of its educational facets and procedures from this level even though junior high students are not ready for such later adolescent activities. High schools especially, in the eleventh and twelfth grade, are dealing with people who are largely people still seeking adult status and privileges.

In conclusion, it must be asked to what degree will the intermediate and middle school concepts actualize educational programs based upon the characteristics and needs of early adolescents instead of the adoption of high school approaches developed in junior high schools? A growing number of schools are effectively meeting this challenge and overcoming operational problems with varying success. Their successes provide us with the inevitable procedure schools must identify and pursue if, indeed, they are sincerely concerned with improving education for their emerging adolescent population.

1. Identify and study the characteristics and needs of the emerging adolescent learner group in your local school-community setting.

2. Develop a curricular rationale which will compliment these needs in this setting.

3. Organize an administrative vehicle to expedite this program toward a planned articulation of your community's total K-12 educational program.

Working to personalize the educative experience of the emerging adolescent requires cooperative planning among teachers and supportive staff involved with a given group of students. The marshalling of all the resources available to the teaching team through such planning is paramount. Fortunately, we have arrived at a point when the increase in the number of schools who have actualized such procedures gives us a greater opportunity to learn how they have achieved this task as a means for improving instruction for their emerging adolescent population. Likewise, the literature of curriculum planning and education at the junior high/

middle school level now can provide us with specific departures as we seek to organize such cooperative planning in our school settings. The purpose of this information package will have been achieved if what it has described and referred to can facilitate your school in developing means to help students succeed more effectively in their personal achievement of adolescence. Whether great or limited, the individual child's potential is the only one he has, and thus, there is no heavier burden! ▶

References

Alessi, S.J., & Toepfer, C.F., Jr. (1971). Home base teaching—guidance in the middle school: The teacher—counselor team. *Dissemination Services on the Middle Grades, II* (7),1-4.

Alexander, W., Williams, E., Compton, M., Hynes, V., & Prescott, D. (1967). *The Emergent Middle School.* New York: Holt, Rinehart and Winston, Inc.

Anderson, R. (1966). *Teaching in a World of Change.* New York: Harcourt, Brace and World.

Bair, M., & Woodward, R. (1964). *Team Teaching in Action.* Boston: Houghton Mifflin Company.

Beggs, D. (Ed.). (1966). *Team teaching – Bold new venture.* Bloomington, IN: University Press.

Chamberlain, L. (1969). *Team Teaching Organization and Administration.* Columbus, OH: Charles E. Merrill.

Committee on adolescence, Group for the Advancement of Psychiatry, Calvin F. Settlage, Chairman (1968). *Normal adolescence.* New York: Charles Scribner's Sons.

Forbes, G. (1968). Physical aspects of early adolescence. In Thomas Curtis (Ed.), *The Middle School* (pp. 25-41). Albany, NY: State University of New York.

Gorden, I. (1969). *Human Development from Birth Through Adolescence.* New York: Harper and Row.

Maslow, A. (1964). *Motivation and Personality.* New York: Harper & Row.

Perrone, P., Ryan, T.A., & Zeran, F. (1970). *Guidance and the emerging adolescent.* Scranton, PA: International Textbook Company.

Toepfer, C.F., Jr. (1969). Home base teaching—Guidance every day for every student. *Operational Briefing. Croft Middle School/Junior High Principal's Service, I* (3), 1-4.

Toepfer, Jr., C.F., & Rosenbaum, D. (1966). *Curriculum planning and school psychology: The coordinated approach.* Cambridge Springs, PA: Hertillon Press.

Verduin, Jr., J. (1967). *Cooperative Curriculum Improvement.* Englewood Cliffs, NJ: Prentice-Hall, Inc..

Challenge to Middle School Education: Preventing Regression to the Mean

Published in *Middle School Journal*, September, 1976

T he rising ground-swell of intellectual, as well as economic, retrenchment challenging American education is critical. We must plan both strategic and tactical means to develop a public understanding of the real successes of our middle school programs. In our desire to extend our success to date, we must be careful not to lose all that has been achieved for our youngsters in the middle school movement during the past twenty years. I do believe, however, that we can meet this challenge and show our constituencies what effective middle school programs have achieved beyond the limits of the old junior high preoccupation with second-ary schooling. As an institution, the old junior high school really never put it all together. It usually had the words down pat, but, in most cases, it didn't know the music.

As for the genealogy of the middle school, however, we are certain of its forebears, we know processes involved in its creation, and in some districts of the use of the shotgun to finalize the affair!

We have the obligation to study carefully the aspects of programs which have proven successful in the best of the nation's middle schools, assess local district needs, and then carefully develop the most appropriate means to meet locally defined needs. We must do this, also, to discredit the negative voices of the back-to-basics advocates. We are in a time which requires speaking out and standing up for what we know is necessary and vital to preserve quality education in the middle grades. It is imperative that we not knuckle under to things which we know will prove detrimental to children.

Unfortunately, there are already increasing numbers of communi-ties in which the winds of backlash are attacking at will anything which varies from the profile of the American public school of 1930. We ourselves have need to really understand the back-to-basics rationale. I would recommend to each of you the article by Van Til, Brownson, and Hamm (1975), entitled "Back to Basics—With a Difference." They identify the back-to-basics movement as the manifest frustrations of parents and adults afraid for their children because the family unit can no longer control, through its own means, the socialization of its young. The school, of course, is a sitting duck for their anguish. The article builds a highly convincing case around the sole alternative for schools being the identification of how schools are exerting positive influences and actually working for the betterment of children.

The roles and processes of the middle school are best captured for me in a rather odd source. My concept of the ideal role for the middle school and its staff, as well as the needs which children bring to us there are beautifully stated by the late Lebanese poet, Kahlil Gibran (1923), in his piece, "On Children."

> Your children are not your children,
>> They are the sons and daughters of life's longing for itself.
>> They come through you but not from you;
>> And though they are with you yet they belong not to you .
>
> * * *
>
> You may give them your love but not your thoughts
>> For they have their own thoughts.
>> You may house their bodies but not their souls,
>> For their souls dwell in the house of tomorrow, which you
> cannot visit, not even in your dreams.
>> You may strive to be like them, but seek not to make them
> like you
>> For life goes not backward nor tarries with yesterday.
>> You are the bow from which your children, as living
> arrows, are sent forth.
>> The Archer sees the mark upon the path of the infinite,
> and He bends you with His might that His arrows may go
> swift and far.
>> Let your bending in the Archer's hand be for gladness
>> For even as He loves the arrow that flies, so He loves also
> the bow that is stable. (pp. 18-19)

In these lines the essence of the responsibility we have for children in the middle school is well stated. We can give them our love, guidance, lead them to knowledge, and help them to learn. However, the middle school should not be preoccupied with merely furnishing answers from content. We should help learners to frame their most appropriate questions and then help them seek answers. The role for us in the middle school to help children prepare for their future is clear in the concept of *Future Shock*. The destiny of the middle school learned is truly in the house of tomorrow, and while there is help we can provide him today, the 1976 model is not what he can best use in his future world of change. I see the middle school and its teachers as the bow to which Gibran refers. Providing that fine balance of flexibility and stability in the bow is imperative in our role in educating our students and thrusting them forward on their inevitable journey into ensuing school, life, and social future.

What is it that we must preserve and nourish in the middle school movement? Essentially, there is a spirit and attitude which we must not lose. In addition, we can identify aspects of program which we can observe in the outstanding middle schools of the nation. The mean to which we dare not regress also holds an attitude. We cannot fall back to a time when almost anything was good enough to cast into the middle grades as early secondary schooling. If you couldn't make it in the elementary or high school, you would gather by the waters of the junior high. We dare not regress to those days. This is not to infer that the junior high was a total failure by any means. It was, and still is possible to identify outstanding, individual junior high schools with highly effective programs based upon the characteristics and needs of emerging adolescent learners. However, the middle school concept gives us promise of institutionalizing a school unit based upon those developmental and learning needs of students formerly achieved in only that minority of excellent junior high schools. To this end, the middle school has developed upon the premise that schools serving emerging adolescents must differ from both elementary and high schools to serve adequately the educational requisites of their population.

The literature and research confirms that an encouraging measure of this promise has been fulfilled. While the beginnings of the middle school movement are almost twenty years old, the phenomenon as a national movement has largely flourished within the past decade. We have evidence that increasing numbers of middle schools are meeting more effectively the intellectual, personal, and social needs of the children they serve. These data refer to progress in the very best of what we now know as middle schools. Unfortunately, far too many others have merely taken on the name, "middle school," while extending their secondary school orientation down to include grades five or six. It is important, then, that these "middle-schools-in-name-only" examine the successes of true middle schools and identify how they can now move from a basis of schooling to one of education for their students.

Essential ingredients for outstanding middle schools

Eight elements which I have found as consensus ingredients in nationally recognized, outstanding middle schools are presented as benchmarks which all middle schools might utilize in examining their programs.

1. Uniqueness of the middle school learner

Outstanding middle schools place primary importance upon stating learner characteristics in terms of local prerogatives. This should reflect local study of middle grade learner characteristics and identify how educational and personal needs of this group differ from those of both elementary and high school students. These statements of learned characteristics help communicate appropriate concerns to parents, laymen, and the professional staff. Obviously, it is easy for any "junior-high-wolf-in-sheep's clothing" to lift any such statement wholesale from another system and palm it off as his own. This merely delays the necessary first step of identifying local learner needs and characteristics. It must be clearly understood that any real success in developing an educational program based upon learner needs requires an identification of the realities of life in a particular school community. Baseball players learned long ago that you can't steal first base!

2. Curricular rationale for the local middle school

The second area of consensus among leading middle schools appears to grow sequentially from the first. Given the statements of locally defined characteristics of the middle grades age group, the school program then needs to become a curricular rationale designed to support the needs of your learners. Learning strategies, instructional approaches, and the entire middle school program must be planned as a curricular rationale in a means-ends continuum. This contrasts sharply with those situations which avoid local definition of learner needs and launch quickly into the latest innovative bandwagon that is in current educational vogue. While all such approaches have proven effective in particular circumstances in themselves they are likely to be of little abstract merit. Such poorly-defined efforts usually result in the curricular rationale going around like an accident looking for a place to happen.

3. General education

Outstanding middle schools have not lost sight of the fact that the middle unit of the American school system continues to have a primary responsibility for general education. The effective middle school must help its learners internalize those skills, facts, and information necessary for all children to know in order to function in our society. Learning how to learn and the development of individual social, intellectual, and living skills must constitute the fabric of the educational experience provided by the middle school. All too many ineffective middle schools have cast aside the goals of general education as obsolete. They have substituted new programs in which mastery of subject matter in and of itself supercedes all else. The effectiveness of such approaches even in the high school has never been actually validated. Its extension downward into the middle grades, however, is totally contrary to the goals of the middle school movement. The success of outstanding middle schools in teaching basic skills as part of a sound, general education program should reinforce those of us being intimidated by the "back-to-basic-education" advocates and the dehumanizing threat they pose to our children.

4. Exploration

Outstanding middle schools continue to develop innovative exploratory programs which help learners explore their personal needs and interests. These programs are provided, not only in "traditional" exploratory areas of art, music, home economics, and industrial arts, but in other areas. Mini-course and activity programs provide additional facets for exploration by learners. A most positive consensus thrust occurs when the mode of instruction within the general education, academic, and elective course offering take on an exploratory emphasis. Certainly, the middle school child needs increased opportunities for self-definition through exploratory education. These opportunities are critical if the emerging adolescent is to find out who he really is and what he might like to become.

5. Focus upon individual growth

A common earmark among outstanding middle schools is their provision of means for individual growth. This has been facilitated through efforts to personalize learning. These efforts have minimized the measurement and reporting of learning upon group norms alone. As a result, student progress has become much more visible on a continuum in terms of individual student skills, interests, and abilities rather than locked into pre-defined grouping based solely upon achievement ability perimeters. Leading middle schools have developed sequence patterns in which not all children must learn the same information even at differing rates. Where backgrounds and capabilities of individual students warrant, they are exempted from some sequences in favor of alternative programs, with options or extended study in areas of their personal interest or need. This is a far cry from the majority of middle school programs where each student must experience the same program on a self-paced basis and his learning reported by some kind of group progress device. Unfortunately, such schools have yet to discover the true meaning of individual differences!

6. Maximization of cooperative planning

Outstanding middle schools have realized that there is nothing intrinsically magical about team teaching. Various formalized team teaching approaches exist in these schools but only as an outgrowth of cooperative planning activities. Their concern is to provide the greatest possible amount of cooperative planning time among groups of teachers sharing the same student population. While cooperative planning time has proven essential where team teaching has flourished, similar cooperative planning time is necessary for teachers operating in other instructional modes. Recognition is increasing that a variety of instructional modes, including departmentalization, teaming, differentiated staffing, self-containment, all are necessary to utilize the strengths of an entire faculty and to match best learner and teacher styles. The learning styles of middle grades children differ so widely that no one single instructional mode can effectively accommodate all students in any one middle school. The objective here is to facilitate cooperative planning among teachers to the greatest possible degree. The effectiveness of all instructional strategies and tactics thus can be greatly improved.

7. Concern with improving student self-concept

The increasing incidence of suicide, alcoholism, addictive syndromes, and mental illness among older children requires that the middle school pay much greater attention to helping students develop a realistic and positive self-concept. Leading middle schools have reorganized pupil personnel services to help teachers better understand the nature, characteristics, and problems of their learner population. In addition, these supportive services have been brought into planning configurations with teachers to make their expertise more readily available throughout the middle school program. Most school programs still relegate these specialists to their offices and do not facilitate full interaction and planning between counselors and teachers. In lighthouse middle schools, however, these services have not been curtailed, despite economic conditions, or boxed off. The high visibility which these services have gained and the importance parents now place upon them is the result.

8. Articulation of middle with elementary and high school programs

Success in our best middle schools has been based upon improved articulation of the middle school with the elementary and high school programs within the district. Changes in the middle grades have been part of systematic, K-12, district-wide, curriculum planning. Changes in program for the middle grades have been finalized only after study of the possibilities of reorganization which affect elementary and high school programs. Where necessary, changes have been made in the elementary program to provide children with the experience they will need to take greatest advantage of improvements in the middle school program. While the high school remains the "hardest nut to crack" there is considerable evidence in better districts that high schools are reorganizing aspects of their programs to take greater advantage of the increased skills and learning which students have gained from the improved program in the middle grades. This is an important point to be recognized in those districts where changes in middle school programs occur without any awareness at either elementary or high school levels. Such myopic changes in the middle school only serve to weaken whatever district-wide articulation of program still may exist. Certainly, such actions serve to increase the frustration of students who now will have wider gaps to span in moving from one school unit to the next.

Conclusion

There is no "add-water-and-stir" nostrum intended here. Certainly, there are other factors which tend to separate leading from mediocre middle schools. However, these eight areas do constitute the consensus elements in which outstanding middle schools have concurred. The middle school movement has reached a point where the reasons for success and failure both need careful study. It is also high time that we specify how and why successful middle school programs have made a difference for learners from the old, institutionalized junior high concept. To this end, our "middle-schools-in-name-only" had better either "fish" or "cut bait!" These eight consensus areas are recommended as appropriate points on which to begin this critical investigation. If nothing else, it should be helpful to identify how your middle school rates in these categories, and . . . if it doesn't, to find out why not!

Perhaps, this all boils down to identifying what it is we really should be trying to do for children in the middle grades. Certainly, no monolithic structure is implied here. Different outstanding middle schools have developed different means to reach their success even within the eight categories discussed here.

I can assure that your program will regress if it moves into change for the sake of change. To switch blithely, for instance, from departmentalization to team teaching with no staff or community understanding of the need for such a change merely plays into the hands of the "back-to-basics" critics. In fact, you will be helping them look good in their criticisms.

Effective curriculum change has always taken time. To look for short-cuts or instant change in the middle school is a crucial error. Beware of the light at the end of a strange tunnel – it might be a locomotive coming your way.

One principle should be evident: systematic curriculum planning on a district-wide basis is the only consistent way to refine the middle school program and avoid the regression syndrome which lurks around us. If the middle school movement slips and loses its foothold on the hillside of progress, the chances of surviving the probable avalanche are slim. However, no one ever said the task would be easy. If we fail to plan adequately, we must then bear full responsibility for whatever regression occurs.

The magnificent opportunity we have is a challenge to invest our minds, hopes, and best professional efforts in making the middle school all that it might be. Certainly, there is no question who we must pay. We pay our dues daily to each emerging adolescent youngster who comes to us wanting to learn and looking for his pathway into the fantastic future.

May our bow be flexible but stable. May our bending in the hand of the Archer be for gladness. Because of our concern, may His arrows go swift and far. ❯

References

Van Til, W., Brownson, W., & Hamm, R. (1975). Back to basics – With a difference. *Educational Leadership*, October, 8-13.

Gibran, K. (1923). *The Prophet*. New York: Alfred A. Knopf, Inc.

Conrad F. Toepfer, Jr. reflects...

Preparing Today's Young Adolescents to Succeed in Tomorrow's World

T he author has developed this piece around what he believes to be the emerging central challenge to middle level educa- tion at the dawning of 1998 – educating moral citizens who can responsibly participate in democratic society. It stems from his observation that hopes for the survival of the "Good Society" have diminishing chances unless our schools develop effective, moral citizens. Preparing young adolescents with academic skills for continued learning will have limited value unless we first help them to become moral citizens and intelligent participants in democratic life.

Building upon their childhood experiences, most people largely fashion their attitudes about learning and work, as well as their enduring adult values between 10 and 15 years of age. Relatively few people substantially change their beliefs in those attributes after reaching high school (Toepfer, Arth, Bergmann, Brough, Clark, Johnston, 1993). The Carnegie Task Force on the Education of Young Adolescents (Carnegie, 1989) stated that "the middle level school years are the last best chance for early adolescents to avoid a diminished future" (p. 8). They further noted:

> Unfortunately, by age 15, substantial numbers of American youth are at risk of reaching adulthood unable to meet adequately the requirements of the workplace, the commitments of relationships in families and with friends, and the responsibilities of participation in a democratic society. These youth are among the estimated 7 million young people – one in four adolescents – who are ex- tremely vulnerable to multiple, high risk behaviors and school failure. Another 7 million may be at moderate risk but remain a cause for serious concern. (p.8)

The high school years are too late to begin helping youth overcome the difficulties confronting them. Yet, today's tightening of educational dollars raises regrettable possibilities. For example, if necessary, this writer would endorse the following action. Excise programs that belatedly address problems in high school and reallocate those finances to support earlier programs designed to alleviate those problems.

The onslaught against education and youth services

The current onslaught on education and youth services by the federal and state legislatures in the name of decreasing governmental budgets is at best obscene and shortsighted. Yet, where is the voice of middle level educational leaders and agencies to stem and reverse this rising tide? It is tragic that so many of those who widely advocated what is "good for kids" in noncontroversial times now stand mute against the increasing legislative onslaught on education and youth support. In their need to be politically correct, the ranks of such fair weather friends of youth swell as they look away from their obligation to confront school, curriculum, and school program implications of social issues engulfing our youth.

The media continues to jump on the "cut-educational-spending" bandwagon. In their "rush" to "out-Limbaugh" each other, radio and television talk-show demagogues across the nation proliferate the media with attacks on what is popularly viewed as wasteful expenditures on education and youth-serving agencies. The actual margin of victory the new legislators claimed in November 1994 was not overwhelming. In fact, only 39 percent of eligible voters in the United States voted in those national and state elections. Twenty percent of them endorsed the candidates of the right, and 18 percent supported the incumbents and other candidates. Hardly a landslide, the new legislators view this as a mandate to uproot the social and educational institutions serving the poor and the youth of the nation. The legislative onslaught against education and our youth has decimated those services with further retrenchments promised.

From an educational and social service perspective, the "Contract With America" seems to be more of a "Contract *On* America's

Youth." For example, why the blanket move to curtail school lunch programs? If abuses did provide lunches for some non-needy youth, why not correct the abuses instead of making cuts across those programs? Poor children do not have the means to purchase school meals that others have from their family resources. At best, such rushes to judgment by the new political leadership are cruel and punitive. Would the majority of our citizens actually vote for such draconian assaults on youth?

Those who disagree with the current initiatives now need to come forth, organize, and take that case to our local, regional, and national public. The long-term fiscal and social dangers being created by current short-term, shortsighted savings must be made crystal clear. The next major national elections will take place in the year 2000, the advent of the third millennium. If the majority of the electorate endorse the merits of what is currently being done to our nation's educational and social services, so be it!

The risks posed to youth by the current initiatives need to be clearly identified and broadly promulgated. In his April 1996 address at State University of New York at Buffalo, University of California Los Angeles Professor Richard McLaren stated that "today youth are living a constant state of emergency." The declining stability of the family and other institutions that historically engaged in rearing and nurturing youth has increasingly placed that responsibility on education and youth services. It is now absolutely critical that we adequately finance schools and youth-serving institutions. If we allow the cutting of middle level school programs and supports we will reduce the chance of today's young adolescents for educational success in high school and beyond.

The increasing numbers of our elderly make it imperative that they become aware of the need to support education and youth services. All our adult citizens need to understand the changes in the structures of the contemporary American family (Johnston, 1990) and their implications for today's youth. Increasing numbers of middle level and high school youth face extenuating out-of-school responsibilities and problems.

For example, increasing numbers of high school and middle school students have obligations to get younger siblings (and for some, their own children) to school. Since middle schools often open earlier than district elementary schools, young adolescents with such responsibilities may be late getting to school. Merely extending the school day, the school year, developing Saturday school, and year-round schools, often does not benefit students with such custodial responsibilities. Those arrangements discriminate against the growing numbers of young adolescents with custodial responsibilities to younger siblings, or their own children.

Because of their familial obligations, those individuals cannot stay longer in the school day or come back later to take advantage of extended learning opportunities. Supervised day care services in schools will be required so that students responsible for younger siblings, or for their own children, can gain that help in school. Greater cooperative school/community/societal interaction is essential if schools are to accomplish what changing conditions are demanding of our schools. Such approaches must become the norm if our nation is to move toward societal wellness.

Our obligation to nurture "humanness"

The altruism of youth may be the best hope for improving human quality of life. If that is true, we must not overlook the critical need to nurture the moral dimensions of their "humanness." In 1630 AD, Moravian educational reformer Comenius (Johann Amos Komensky) wrote:

> We are all citizens of one world. We are all of one blood. To hate a man because he was born in another country, because he speaks a different language, or because he takes a different view of this subject or that, is a great folly. Desist, I implore you, for we are all equally human. Let us have but one end in view, the welfare of humanity.

Nurturing humanness requires a concerted effort among all who share in raising children. The West African proverb claims, "a child is so precious that it takes a whole village to raise one." The vanishing of such a shared concern in most communities now

Americans to coalesce in attempting to succeed in that effort. That will require stabilizing and reducing disagreement about the roles and responsibilities of each constituent group in that process. Yet, today, even the roles of our schools and their relationship to the familial and community efforts to rear youth have become blurred. This disharmony is increasingly detrimental to the welfare and well-being of our youth.

Schools face the problem of identifying those values around which public schools should properly be organized. That dilemma revolves around the difficulty of defining some collective value norms as a guide for what we should do in school. That is complicated by increasing disagreement, and in some communities, and even an absence of clearly defined core values in the community itself.

Continuing dramatic changes in contemporary family structure and stability are impacting all of this. More families seem less able, and even unable, to fulfill traditional roles and responsibilities in rearing and nurturing their young. Even if it is less than the collapse of the family some suggest, the dynamic vortex of changes in family structure and stability pose serious problems for increasing numbers of young people.

The stability of marriage and family structure continues to decline. Popenoe and Bethke (1995) reported that in less than three decades, the United States has gone from the world's "most marrying society" to the one with most divorces and unwed mothers. Their data reveal that between 1970 and 1990 the percentage of married American adults decreased from 72 to 62 percent. Less than half of marriages now last a decade. They concluded that this shift has significantly contributed to the deteriorating well-being of American children and youth.

Johnson (1996) reported that 600,000 of the 2,000,000 annual births in our nation are out-of-wedlock and that half those born in cities are out-of wedlock births. There is no category that identifies and records separation and termination of living arrangements by parents of children born out-of-wedlock. Only 38 percent of American school-aged children now live with two (not necessarily original) parents.

Rosemond (1995) noted the projection that only 6 percent of black and 30 percent of white children born in 1980 will live with both biological parents until age 18. He reported that the comparable figures for children born in 1950 were 51 and 81 percent respectively. One in three households in the United States is now headed by a single parent, and nine in ten single-parent families are fatherless; and today, only 23 percent of American children are being raised by two parents (Johnson 1996). Over 40 percent of school-aged children have seen their parents divorce. Over 30 percent have seen their parents separate to either reconcile or remain apart.

Our nation has too long swept the impact of separation and divorce upon children "under the rug." A national longitudinal study published in Spring, 1997, discussed the long-term negative effect of divorce upon children, including their success in school. Jacobson (1997) reported the findings of Wallenstein's twenty-five year research on the psychological effects of divorce on children. It identified a number of areas in which children living with single parents were particularly vulnerable. The emotional damage extends into adulthood.

Children whose parents divorced had lower high school and college completion rates than children whose parents did not divorce. Children of divorce were found to be more vulnerable in dealing with alcohol, drugs, and sex in their early and later adolescence. They were sexually active earlier and, as adults themselves, had significantly higher incidences of those problems than did children whose parents did not divorce. Those data show that many children need interaction beyond the best quality time that single parents can provide them.

In view of such shifts, parents have an increasing need for programs that can help them and their children deal with these issues. What roles might middle level school programs take on in addressing these concerns? Education has to decide if, and, if so, how it can respond to such needs more youth are bringing to school. Any attempts toward prevention would require developing middle level school experiences that help young adolescents develop greater emotional stability.

The need to engage parents, guardians, and educators in communities grows and compounds. While national statistics confirm the increase in the number of school-aged girls conceiving and bearing children out-of-wedlock (Johnson, 1996), it is imperative to identify local incidences. Even if that proves to be minor locally, families, educators, and the community need to define and agree upon their shared responsibilities to deal effectively with it.

This writer discovered the following in an urban middle level school last year. In that school, only 9 percent of students were living with two parents. In one case, because both their parents were serving life sentences in a state penitentiary, a fifth grade girl and her eighth grade brother were being raised by indigent, seventy-six-year-old and seventy-nine-year-old grandparents. Current welfare legislation in that situation directed both parents' welfare monies to them, not to the grandparents attempting to raise their children. Major reform is desperately needed to correct such obscenities.

While conditions for youth continue to deteriorate across the nation, the suggestion that schools and other community/societal agencies ought to take on greater roles in raising youth triggers a range of arguments. It seems as if the "whole village" is content to disagree while the needs of youth continue to go unaddressed and become compounded. Questions of whose and which values, delivered by what or whom for whose children stalemate any significant amelioration of these problems for youth. In order for schools to significantly help youth, school/communities must work to identify and agree on similar central, societal beliefs and values which are held in that setting.

Moral dilemmas in American democracy

Efforts to respect and accommodate the increasing diversity among Americans focus upon differences among groups. However, we need to identify areas of commonalties and agreements among values to help bridge and articulate that growing diversity. One focus could be to identify central, moral commonalties among belief systems. Most of those belief systems have evolved and been adapted from philosophies and religions. For example, the following moral value of what we now call "The Golden Rule" evolved chronologically from such venerable sources.

From the *Dadistan-i -Dinik* (94:5) of Zoroastrianism (9th century B.C.):
That nature is good which checks itself from doing to others that which would not be good for itself.

From the *Analects* of Confucianism (6th century B.C.):
Here certainly is the golden maxim. Do not do to others that which we do not want them to do to us.

From the *Udana-Varga* (3-18) of Hinduism (3rd century B.C.):
Such is the sum of duty; do not do to others that which would do harm to yourself.

From Jainist philosophy (5th century, B.C.):
In happiness and suffering, in joy and grief, we should regard all creatures as we regard our own self.

From Classical Paganism, Plato (4th century B.C.):
May I do to others as would that they should do unto me.

From the Sabbat (21a) in the *Talamud* of Judiasm (5th century B.C.):
That which you hold detestable, do not do to your neighbor. That is the whole law; the rest is commentary.

From the Gospel According to St. Matthew (7:12) in the Christian *New Testament* (1st century A.D.):
All things you would have people do to you, you should do unto them. This is the law of the prophets.

From the *Tai Shang Kan Ying Pian* of Taoism (1st century B.C.):
Consider that your neighbor gains your gain, and that your neighbor loses that which you lose.

From the Sunna in the *Koran* of Islam (13th century A.D.):
None of you is a believer if he does not desire for his brothers what he desires for himself.

From Sikhism (16th century A.D):
Treat others as you would be treated yourself.

From Rationalist philosophy, Immanuel Kant (18th century A.D.):
Act in such a way that you always treat humanity, whether in your own person or in the person of any other, never simply as a means, but always at the same time, an end.

John Paul II's focus on moral values in *Crossing The Threshold of Hope* (1994) made it a "best seller" among Christians and non-Christians alike. Conversely, the large percentages of American Roman Catholics sampled (Sheler, October 9, 1995) disagreed with the Pope's positions on birth control and women's rights. However, his last visit to the United States confirmed his personal recognition as a leader in the cause for furthering human rights. Could such concerns of the American population at-large regarding improvement of the moral condition in contemporary society stem from their assumptions about the tenets of life in a democracy?

The moral dimension of democracy is rooted in the equal treatment of humanity. The United States has long ascribed to the ideal of "E Pluribus Unum" (One Out of Many). However, accelerating cultural, ethnic, and racial diversification among Americans has complicated the task of keeping a leveled playing field for all of our citizens. To advance the reality of "E Pluribus Unum" in our nation, as adults, today's young adolescents will have to improve upon the actions of present adults regarding the values issues facing our diversifying nation. Today's young adolescents must gain both the will and the skill needed to resolve growing divisiveness within our nation. If not, the "Balkanization" of a shift toward "Pluribus E Pluribus" (Many Out of Many) could move our nation from a Republic toward a Confederation. We must not underestimate the need for parents and schools to agree on how best to deal with values issues in educating today's young adolescents.

The moral possibilities of democracy in the United State are seen as characterizing the central appeal of life in our nation. Granted, opportunities for greater material quality of life attracted many to become American citizens over the past 200- some years. Yet, this writer believes that the goodness people across the globe have perceived in our nation may have caused even more people to become Americans. If so, the keystone in that attraction is what people view as the value tenets of American democracy. Those principles focus upon the rights of individuals and of the society at-large. Millions have come here for the promise of a freedom that in fulfilling one's rights: (1) individuals may neither infringe on the rights of other individuals nor on the welfare of society at large; (2) society at large may not infringe the freedom of individuals to pursue their rights in such a manner; and, (3) that problems arising within that society shall be justly decided for the welfare of both individuals citizens and the general societal good.

Life in contemporary America requires that youth understand what will be required of them to move society toward a higher moral destiny. Again, this seems particularly important during the years of early adolescence. In his address to the annual conference of the National Middle School Association, J. Howard Johnston (1994) discussed the need for middle level educators to help young adolescents understand and develop citizenship behaviors they need now and as adults. As examples he stated that our young adolescents need to understand that:

1. It is wrong to discriminate on the bases of gender, race, ethnicity, and gender.
2. It is wrong to do violence to other people.
3. It is good to treat other people with compassion, fairness, and integrity.

Any serious attempts to assist youth in stabilizing and reversing the growing instances of violent behaviors in today's youth and adult society must be grounded in such understandings.

The schools and values education dilemma

Controversy continues to rage as to whether or not American public education should deal with values issues. However, why should schools *not* participate in considering, modeling, and even orienting youth toward such issues? The values of the vast numbers of teachers are well within the range of those of the community. As Johnston (1994) further commented, "very few teachers, probably less than in any societal group, are either Nazis or raving libertines." Why, then do communities feel it necessary to muzzle schools and educators while allowing every other group its First Amendment of the Constitution freedom to spout its messages without inhibitions?

There are indications that the public is beginning to see the need for schools to deal with values issues. The Public Agenda Foundation (1994) conducted a wide public survey before issuing its report *First Things First: What Americans Expect From Their Public Schools.* The executive summary of that report stated:

> People want schools to teach values. They especially want schools to emphasize those values that allow a diverse society to live together peacefully. The public's lack of concern about "values issues" does not mean that Americans endorse education that is "value-neutral" or makes no judgments about moral behavior. There is a circle of broadly agreed upon values people expect the schools both to teach directly and to reinforce by example. And, there are some "lessons" that most Americans believe are not the business of the public schools — those that seem aimed at dividing people rather than helping them live in harmony. (p. 2)

Noddings (1995) discussed the need for a "morally defensible mission for schools in the 21st century." She saw the following tenets as major in that attempt.

> The main aim of education should be to produce competent, caring, loving, and lovable people. We should discuss the essential questions – including spiritual matters – freely. Moreover, we need to help students learn to treat each other ethically by giving them practice in caring. (p. 368)

Meier (1994) identified how schools can help students develop the skills to move the initiatives of democracy ahead in contemporary America. Those approaches were developed and initiated in New York City's District 4 Model. She noted:

> A democratic society has the right to insist that the central function of schooling is to cultivate the mental and moral habits that a modern democracy requires. These include openness to other viewpoints, the capacity to sustain uncertainty, the ability to act on partial knowledge, and the inclination to step into the shoes of others – all habits that can be uncomfortable to have but, it is hoped, hard to shake. Until we face the fundamental question of the purpose of schooling, it makes little sense to keep asking for better tools to measure what we haven't agreed about. "What's it for?" the young ask often enough. It's time adults took the question seriously. There are no silver bullets when it comes to raising children right, no fast-track solutions with guaranteed cures. The only sensible course involves hard work, keeping your eye on the prize, and lots of patience for the disagreements that inevitably arise. (p. 373)

Young adolescents need to see their teachers model clear and explicit value positions, however, *whose* values? Johnston (1994) suggested that we deal with community values, ones like the following:

> Hard work pays, even in an unfair world.

> Treat others with the same respect and dignity with which you would like to be treated

> You feel better when you do what's right, rather than evading your moral precepts. (p. 14)

This writer suggests it is both reasonable and essential that schools and teachers be given opportunities to engage with youth as the latter consider value goals in today's difficult times. The modeling of positive behaviors and discussing the needs for such values in school can do much to balance the negative values youth observe in other dimensions of life. Even with the variance of educator's positions, their addressing values issues would be far more positive and much less harmful, for example, than the unbridled and unmonitored viewing of regular and cable television by most school-aged youth.

Bridging societal dissonance

Dissonant and violent human interactions make it necessary that middle level schools find ways that prepare young adolescents to address such concerns now and in their adult futures. The changes inundating the lives of students present major challenges to our schools. Life and the media increasingly pound children with desensitizing images of violence, drugs, and other worrisome things.

The problem is manifested in violence upon youth, violence by youth against society, citizens at-large, and upon themselves. Homicide is now the second, and suicide is the third leading cause of death among age eleven- through eighteen-year-old American youth. Homicide is the leading cause in urban settings (Wolff, Rutten, & Bayers, 1992).

Yet, where is the support that schools require to become the safe, well-disciplined places that the national educational goals have directed them to become? Ironically, in April 1995 the United States Supreme Court ruled that gun-free zones around schools were illegal and could no longer be enforced. The tragedy of youth shootings has not apparently made a point of law.

Johnson (1996) identified that each day, an average of 35 school-aged youth in our nation now die from gunfire and that shootings by school-aged youth have tripled in the last decade. Yet, more states are passing laws allowing citizens to carry concealed weapons.

At the end of the school day last December 1st, a 14-year-old high school freshman opened fire with a hand gun on fellow students kneeling in the lobby of West Padukah, Kentucky's Heath High

School. He did not disclose the reason for killing three and critically wounding five of his school mates. When will schools and their communities see their need to interface their efforts working to counteract and reduce youth violence?

The suggestion that educational agendas should address such conditions is not a new one. Over a quarter-century ago, Mumford (1951) stated:

> The transformation of hate and aggressiveness into kindness, of destructiveness into life-furthering activities depends upon our discovering the formative principle that prevails during the period of growth and development. So, the withdrawal of love and the rise of aggression go hand in hand; for love is the capacity for embracing otherness, for widening the circle of interests in which the self may operate. (p. 2)

This writer's dear friend, Louis Raths, devoted most of his celebrated career to helping educators address such concerns in the lives of youth. In his last major work Raths (1972) wrote the following to teachers and parents about what he saw as the educational implications of Mumford's concerns.

> In the schoolrooms of the world, and in the homes of the world, what can teachers and parents do which would most likely contribute significantly to the fulfillment of life? What contributes most to that inward calm which we frequently call a sense of well-being? What can we do that will add to the probability that this generation of children will be more zestful, more spontaneous, more cooperative, more thoughtful and considerate of others, more ardent guardians and champions of freedom for everyone?

> What can we do now that will enable this generation of children to have greater control over themselves? As the result, in part, of our efforts, will they be more likely to come to terms with their own impulses, their own inner torments, and griefs? Will they expect too much of

themselves and of their peers? Will they want what they cannot have, and will they reject that which is good for humankind, individually and collectively?

It is your professional obligation to help your children grow, to learn, to mature. The meeting of needs is not your sole responsibility. But, if unmet needs are getting in the way of a child's growth and development, her/his learning and maturing, I insist that it is your obligation to try and meet those needs. I say that with conviction.

I believe it from the bottom of my heart! And so do you, probably. I'm pretty sure that if a child needed glasses you would take some steps to help meet that need. And if a child had some difficulty in hearing you might make many efforts to help meet that need. And so also with their unmet emotional needs.

Children cannot check their emotions at the door, and we should not expect them to do that. We should be very much concerned about their feelings. I have also suggested a child's need to make choices. I have indicated my concerns for a richer curriculum, one that provides for individual differences, and one that gives *all* children chances to succeed and to have feelings of achievement. (pp. 2-3)

The kinds and degrees of difficulties youth face continue to increase. This writer believes middle level education has an obligation of protective custody to respond to those concerns. The success of our efforts will significantly influence how well tomorrow's adults deal with evolving values challenges.

A value base for educational considerations

Kelley (1962) prophetically foresaw many of the youth problems that are now engulfing us. Unfortunately, the challenges to values issues he eloquently voiced continue to go unanswered.

I have heard people who are good friends of youth say that we simply cannot afford the burden of good schools. This is nonsense. The people in the richest country in the world *(in 1997, the United States is the third most wealthy country in the world])* buy what they want. It is only a question as to what they value. I believe that we in education should not concede that the American people cannot afford a well-educated classroom for each twenty-five of their young. We just have to care more about that than something else.

I have mentioned the above items because it seems to me that they are growing symptoms of an increase in the rejection of our own young, and will make the "youth problem," which is really an adult problem, worse instead of better. We can go on, of course, making our society more hostile and more rejecting of our young, but at an awful price. The price will be in more delinquency, more youth violence, more mental hospitals, more police, more juvenile courts. To summarize, I hold that we adults must keep these points in mind.

1. Our culture is in jeopardy unless we can adequately care for our young.
2. Our young are all right when we get them. If all is not well with them, it is due to what has happened to them in an adult-managed world.
3. If youth have not been too badly damaged by the life that has been thrust upon them, they enjoy and desire a good society as much as we do.
4. In urban society, our young live under more difficult circumstances than they used to.
5. The amount of juvenile delinquency in any community is a measure of that community's lack of concern for its young.

6. There is really no valid, responsible place in our urban communities for youth. They are a displaced segment of our society.
7. A place must be made for them, and it seems to me that the only feasible place is the school.

Since nearly everybody believes that the "youth problem" is getting worse as the years go by (and this certainly seems to me to be so), it should be logical to admit that we must be doing something wrong or neglecting something we should do. Let us try something different, something which seems dictated by the findings of researchers. Let us try:

Acceptance of all our young as worthy, valuable, uniquely blessed with some gifts.

Making school a real youth institution.

Involving youth in what is to be undertaken.

Choices for youth, for the development of free, creative, minds.

Cooperation and democracy in place of authoritarianism.

The human approach, rather than stressing those things which lie outside the learner.

Love, to replace the alienation of so many of our own flesh and blood.

The importance of our own credibility as exemplars of consistency and how we conduct ourselves with each other and with them cannot be underestimated. Youth need more models than critics. The process of growing up is basically the process of making mistakes and learning from them. Raising the current priority for the moral and ethical education of young adolescents will require interaction of school personnel with parents, families, and the community. The demands facing youth should define the roles and responsibilities for schools in dealing with values issues.

The reality of life in our shrinking world should also temper that planning. One such issue is the need for equal access to the livable and life-sustaining resources of our planet. There are currently six billion people on earth. It is estimated that number will increase to ten billion people by the year 2040 A.D. Every day, the United States now uses over half of the life-sustaining resources available on the planet. That will change in terms of the demands which the rest of the inhabitants of our planet will increasingly make. Thus youth need to be prepared to function collaboratively in terms of the changes which occur during their lifetimes. Beane, Toepfer, & Alessi (1986) offered one frame schools might consider in trying to prepare today's youth to move from a past – to a futures-loaded perspective.

From > > > > > > > > > > >	To
Reactive Planning	*Proactive Planning*
Present Gratification	*Concern for the Future*
Competition	*Interdependence*
Competitive Distribution of Wealth, Power, and Resources	*Equitable Distribution of Wealth, Power, Resources*
Acquisition of Information	*Use of Information for the Social Good*
Conspicuous Consumerism	*"Enoughness" Consumption*
Hierarchical Power	*Participatory Consensus*
Centralization of Power	*Problem-Solving Networks*
Linear Thinking	*Systemic Thinking*
Conformity to Norms	*Promotion of Diversity*
Emphasis on Science	*Balance Among Science, Perception, and Intuition*
Dependence on Technology	*Selective Use of Technology for Human Purposes*
Unlimited Growth Potential	*Selective Planned Growth*

(p. 395)

The foregoing is only one such approach. Clearly, school/communities have to identify ways to prepare youth for values decisions they face now and will confront in their futures.

Conclusion

In summary, this writer believes that middle level education's primary concern should be to help young adolescents become good citizens with a sense of moral/social values adequate to the challenges of life in our changing world. Lacking that, "the good society" cannot stabilize and endure. Without that foundation, our attention to schooling concerns such as development of young adolescent literacy in language, mathematics, science, and information processing, as well as preparation of students for employability, seems myopic and without foundation.

Data clearly confirm that conditions for youth in contemporary society are not getting better. The chances of their reaching personal, economic self-sufficiency and gaining the skills to become good citizens diminish daily. Wright-Edelman (1992) concludes her book with Ina Hughes' poignant poem describing the problems facing growing numbers of our youth.

We pray for children who sneak popsicles before supper, who erase holes in math workbooks, who can never find their shoes.

And we pray for children who stare at photographers from behind barbed wire, who can't bound down the street in a new pair of sneakers, who never "counted potatoes," who are born in places we couldn't be caught dead, who never go to the circus, who live in an X-rated world.

And we pray for children who bring us sticky kisses and fistfuls of dandelions, who hug us in a hurry and forget their lunch money.

And we pray for children who never get dessert, who have no safe blanket to drag behind them, who watch their parents watch them die, who can't find any bread to steal, who don't have any rooms to clean up, whose pictures aren't on anyone's dressers, whose monsters are real.

And we pray for children who spend all of their allowances before Tuesday, who throw tantrums in the grocery store and pick at their food, who like ghost stories, who shove dirty clothes under the bed and never rinse out the tub, who get visits from the tooth fairy, who don't like to be kissed in front of the carpool, who squirm in church or temple and scream in the phone, whose tears we sometimes laugh at, and whose smiles can make us cry.

And we pray for children whose nightmares come in the daytime, who will eat anything, who have never seen a dentist, who aren't spoiled by anybody, who go to bed hungry and cry themselves to sleep, who live and move but have no being.

We pray for children who want to be carried, and for those who must be, for those we never give up on and for those who don't get a second chance. For those we smother ... and for those who will grab the hand of anybody kind enough to offer it.

Consider the challenges with which Raths (1972) concluded his last book.

It has often been said that we live only once, that we don't have a second or a third chance. I wish I could impress more fathers and mothers, more college teachers of education, more teachers generally, and more administrators, that *all* of us have only one childhood to live, and for many of us it is terribly grim and unhappy. Our children need more freedom, more choices, more dedicated concern from intelligent and compassionate adults. They need adults who are concerned about their needs, values, status, thinking, and are trying to help them whenever we are needed.

I hope that all of us will begin to value children more than we ever did before, and I hope that this increased concern of ours will show up in this present generation of children. We can demonstrate, as it has never been demonstrated before, how happy the life of a child can be. What do you think? Will we do it? (pp. 141-142)

In view of the values needs of today's young adolescents, *will* we have the courage and determination to address these concerns Raths raised a quarter-century ago?

A final thought

Along with its honor, being recognized as one of the "Founders" heightens my sense of obligation. This reflection has shown my "Middle-Level-Education-Ghost-of-Times-Past" concerns for the "Middle-Level-Educational-Future." The challenge middle level educators face in trying to overcome the specters of want and ignorance is a mighty one.

In *A Christmas Carol* (Dickens, 1843), when solicitors who came to his place of business seeking donations for the poor at Christmas time, Ebeneezer Scrooge refused, asking if the prisons, treadmills, and workhouses were no longer available for those unable to support themselves? When the solicitors replied that many would rather die than go there, Scrooge dismissed them saying, "If they would rather die then they had better do it and reduce the surplus population" (p. 12).

Later as Scrooge's time with the Ghost of Christmas Present was about to end, those words were turned upon him. Scrooge noticed something at the bottom of the spirit's garment.

> "Forgive me if I am not justified in what I ask," said Scrooge, looking at the Sprit's robe, "But I see something strange, not belonging to yourself, protruding from your skirts. Is it a foot or a claw?"

> "It might be a claw, for the flesh there is upon it," was the Sprit's Sorrowful reply. "Look there!"

> From the foldings of its robe, it brought forth two children; wretched, abject, frightful, hideous, miserable.

They knelt down at its feet and clung upon the outside of its garment.

"Oh, Man! look here. Look, look, down here! exclaimed the Ghost."

They were a boy and girl. Yellow, meagre, ragged, scowling, wolfish; but prostrate, too in their humility. Where graceful youth should have filled their features out, and touched them with its freshest tints, a stale and shriveled hand, like that of age, had pinched, and twisted them, and pulled them into shreds. Where angels might have sat enthralled, devils lurked, and glared out menacing. No change, no degradation, no perversion of humanity, in any grade, through all the mysteries of wonderful creation has monsters so horrible and dread.

Scrooge started back, appalled. Having them shown to him in this way, he tried to say they were fine children, but the words choked themselves, rather than be parties to a lie of such enormous magnitude.

"Spirit! are they yours?"

Scrooge could say no more.

"They are Man's," said the Spirit, looking down upon them. "And they cling to me, appealing from their fathers. This boy is Ignorance. This girl is Want. Beware them both, and all of their degree, but most of all, beware this boy, for on his brow I see that written which is Doom, unless the writing be erased. Deny it!" cried the Spirit, stretching out is hand toward the city. "Slander those who tell it ye! Admit it for your factious purposes, and make it worse. And bide the end!"

"Have they no refuge or resource?" cried Scrooge.

"Are there no prisons?" said the Spirit, turning on him for the last time with his own words. "Are there no workhouses?"

The Bell struck twelve. Scrooge looked around him for the Ghost and saw it not. (pp. 56-57)

Particularly in our rapidly changing times, life must be anticipated in future tense. While young adolescents are now only 25% of the population, they are 100% of the future. As do we all, the National Middle School Association has an awesome responsibility of protective custody for young adolescents. Let us work to fulfill that obligation. ◗

References

Beane, J., Toepfer, C. Jr., & Alessi, S. Jr. (1986). *Curriculum planning and development.* Boston: Allyn and Bacon, Inc.

Carnegie Council on Adolescent Development. (1989). *Turning points: Preparing American youth for the twenty-first century.* Washington, DC: Carnegie Corporation.

Comenius (Komensky), J. (1630). *The labyrinth of the world and the paradise of the heart.* (Translated by C. Lutzow for this 1906 English edition). London: J. M. Dent.

Dickens, C. (1843). *A Christmas carol.* Reprinted in the United States, 1954. New York: Oxford University Press USA.

Jacobson, L. (June 11, 1997). Emotional damage from divorce found to linger. *Education week, 6* (37): 66.

Johnson, C., (1996) *The state of America's children –1966.* Washington, DC.: Children's Defense Fund.

John Paul II. [Edit. V. Messori]. (1994). *Crossing the Threshold of Hope* (translated by J. & M. McPhee). New York: Alfred Knopf, Inc.

Johnston, J. H. (November 5, 1994). *Raising standards, raising children: An agenda for middle school in the 21st century.* Cincinnati, OH: National Middle School Association Annual Conference.

Johnston, J. H. (1990). *The new American family and the school.* Columbus, OH: National Middle School Association.

Kelly, E. (1962). *In defense of youth*. Englewood Cliffs, NJ. Prentice-Hall, Inc.

Meier, D. (1995). How our schools could be. *Phi Delta Kappan, 76* (5): 369-373.

Noddings. N. (1995). A morally defensible mission for schools in the 21st century. *Phi Delta Kappan, 76* (5) 365-368.

Mumford, L. (1951), *The conduct of life*. Harcourt Brace & Company.

Popenoe, D., & Bethke, J. (1995). *Marriage in America: A report to the nation*. Chicago, IL: University of Chicago.

Public Agenda. (1994). *First things first: What Americans want from public schools*. Public Agenda, 6 East Avenue, Suite 900, New York 10016 (Tel. (212- 686-6610, FAX 212-889-3461).

Raths, L. (1972). *Meeting the needs of vhildren: Creating trust and security*. Columbus, OH: Merrill Publishing Company.

Rosemond, J. (1995, June 18). How dads make the difference (syndicated column). *The Buffalo News , E-3*.

Sheler, J., Dimmler, E., Pollak, K., Bennefield, A., Mulrine, A. (1995, October 9). Keeping faith in his time. *US. News & World Reports* 119, (14): 72-75.

Toepfer, C. Jr., Arth, A., Bergmann, S., Brough, J., Clark, D, Johnston, H. (1993). *Achieving excellence through the middle level curriculum*. Reston, VA: National Association of Secondary School Principals.

Wolff, M., Rutten, P., & Bayers, III, A. (1992). *Where we stand: Can America make it in the global race for wealth, health, and happiness?* New York: Bantam Books.

Wright-Edelman, M. (1992). *The measure of our success: A letter to my children and yours*. Boston: Beacon Press. 95-97.

V

Gordon F. Vars

The first two selections published in the mid-sixties demonstrate that I came to the middle school movement from many years spent in teaching and preparing teachers for the junior high school. Since the primary emphasis is on serving the unique educational needs of middle level young people, I see no essential differences in the philosophy and goals of both types of institution.

The third selection is an early version of the curriculum design that I tried to implement as Middle School Coordinator of the Kent State University School. It also provided the structure for the book John Lounsbury and I wrote in 1978, **A Curriculum for the Middle School Years.** *(It still seems reasonable to me!) The last article, published in 1971, attempted to provide some historical perspective on the suddenly popular middle school.*

GORDON F. VARS

Preparing Junior High Teachers

Published in *The Clearning House*, October, 1965

The shortage of well-qualified junior high school teachers is too well-known to require documentation. How can we attract and hold capable people at this level? How can we develop commitment to teaching the young adolescent? What special preparation, if any, should a junior high school teacher have? We have been wrestling with these problems since the first junior high opened around 1910, so it would be presumptuous of me to claim definitive answers now. However, since 1960 the Cornell Junior High School Project has been attempting to attract and to prepare junior high teachers through a fifth-year program for liberal arts graduates, supported by funds from the Ford Foundation. My "prof.'s eye view" of these problems is based primarily on this experience.

Preparation and Certification

Since pre-service preparation is governed to a marked extent by teacher certification requirements, we will examine both at the same time. First, because we want *special preparation* for junior high teaching, it does not necessarily follow that we should have *separate certification* for this level. It is particularly unwise if holders of a junior high certificate can teach only three grade levels. Who would want to limit his job opportunities so narrowly? Consider what is happening in Indiana, for example. A special junior high certificate, restricted to grades seven, eight, and nine, was announced in 1962 and went into effect in September, 1963. As of November, 1964, it was estimated that no more than 50 students in the entire state were working toward that certificate. With 2,500 junior high positions in Indiana, you can see how far this program goes toward meeting the demand for teachers.

Values of Overlapping Certificates.

Instead of closing all other routes to junior high teaching, as suggested by the Indiana certification director. I believe we should more fully exploit the merits of overlapping certificates. Arrangements like Illinois' K through 9 (elementary) and 6 through 12 (secondary) certification continue to be predominant patterns, and for good reason. We need all types of teachers in the junior high school, both the broad generalist typically produced in elementary programs and the subject specialist prepared by most secondary programs. Illinois' four-year overlap is especially desirable in light of number of "Middle Schools" being developed, embracing grades 6, 7, and 8, or even 5 through 8 or 9.

T. H. Briggs cited the elementary-trained teacher's contribution to the junior high as long ago as 1920:

> Their experience in the grades has given them an under-
> standing of boys and girls in early adolescence and has
> made them appreciative of individual differences in
> abilities and sympathetic with any plans that will provide
> for differentiation of work. Whether or not they are by
> large better teachers than others in the school, as many
> maintain, it is unnecessary to consider, for they are
> usually eager to work in the new type of school, while the
> high-school teacher of however humble rank is likely to
> consider his transfer anything but a promotion. (p. 221)

Beginning in 1966, all permanent elementary certificates in New York State will require five years of study and a minimum of 30 semester hours in a department or planned interdepartmental program of liberal arts studies. A special junior high endorsement on this K through 9 certificate is awarded for 36 hours of work in English or social studies, 42 in science, or 24 in mathematics. In addition, at least 80 of the 300 clock hours of supervised teaching must be in the junior high grades.

Unfortunately, no specific work in junior high school education, not even adolescent psychology, is listed as part of the required 30 semester hours in professional education. A junior high endorsement on Indiana's four-year elementary certificate, on the other hand, calls for six semester hours distributed among adolescent psychology, junior high school curriculum and organization, and developmental reading. Indiana also requires 24 hours in a teaching field and two to three semester hours of supervised teaching in the junior high school. These programs are not offered as ideals, but merely to show how elementary certification can be modified to fit at least some of the requirements of junior high teaching.

Another value of elementary type preparation for junior high teachers was identified by Laura McGregor in 1929 when she said: "The experience of having taught all the major subjects of the elementary curriculum leads to a wiser interpretation of departmentalized contents in the light of subject interrelationships, and to a broader comprehension of the problems of other teachers" (p. 271-272). This point is particularly important in view of the number of junior high schools with block-time and core programs – 40 percent at time of the last national survey.

What is needed is modest depth in at least two related fields, such as English and social studies, or science and mathematics. New York and Indiana teachers taking the elementary route to junior certification will be able to qualify in two teaching fields, but this will use up many of their electives. Junior high teachers need more subject matter depth than elementary teachers, but less than senior high teachers.

New York is an example of the ridiculous level of specialization sometimes demanded for secondary certification – 51 semester hours in English or social studies, 57 in science, or 33 in mathematics. This is for a five-year program, of course, but added to general education and professional requirements it leaves little room for breadth, and makes a second teaching field almost impossible. Any state contemplating changes in certification requirements would do well to avoid the mistakes made in New York. Both a teaching major and a teaching minor should be required of all secondary teachers, and especially those planning to work in junior high. The junior high period is much too early for narrow specialization by either teachers or students.

One influence toward specialization some of us view with alarm is teaching. As a long-time advocate of block-time and core, I do not have to be sold on the value of continuous cooperative planning among teachers. But when a team is designed to make one teacher a specialist in grammar, another in composition, and another in literature, for example, we are in danger of re-splintering the curriculum we worked so hard in the 20s and 30s to glue back together through broad fields, block-time, and core curriculum plans.

There is some consolation in David W. Beggs' (1964) statement that "as team operation becomes more sophisticated, it tends to include interdisciplinary membership" (p. 35). Lloyd Trump (1961), too, has illustrated this approach in his writings. Indeed, the interdisciplinary team is receiving increasingly widespread acceptance at both junior and senior high levels. Such a team can promote correlation of subject matter without the overemphasis on one field that sometimes occurs in a block-time program. I have my doubts, however, as to whether the interdisciplinary team can be as effective as block-time in accomplishing other purposes that are particularly important at the junior high level, notably guidance. The point is, whether he will teach a separate subject or block-time, individually or as a member of a team, the junior high teacher should know at least two teaching fields well enough to correlate them whenever appropriate.

Professional Preparation

Work in the teaching of reading and study skills should be required of all teachers, both elementary and secondary. Basic to success in almost any school subject, effective study also may have a special psychological significance for the young adolescent. As Mauritz

Johnson (1962) puts it: "Neither economically nor emotionally can young adolescents become fully independent of adults; given help and increasing opportunity to study effectively on their own, most of them can become academically independent" (p. 58).

Study of adolescent psychology and the role of the teacher in guidance, as sound teaching methods, are commonly conceded to be essential for the junior high teacher. A separate course in junior high school education may be desirable, but not necessary, so long as adequate attention is given somewhere to the history and philosophy of this institution. For many students, a junior high course or seminar will make more sense if taken concurrently with practice teaching, or else immediately afterward, while their junior high experiences are still fresh.

Student Teaching Is Crucial

Since the key to successful junior high teaching lies in how well the teacher works with the age group, professional laboratory experiences with young adolescents are of prime importance. Especially crucial is student teaching, which should take place under teachers who are themselves committed to teaching junior high youngsters. Whether the school in which the teaching takes place should approach the ideal or illustrate more typical practices is a troublesome dilemma. I would not classify schools in which our Junior High School Project interns teach as ideal by any means, yet some of our graduates have experienced real shock at the situations they have encountered after leaving us. On the other hand, if we confront them with grim reality during their practice teaching, they might set their sights too low, missing the vision of what a junior high could be, or even becoming so discouraged as to leave the profession.

Perhaps student teachers should have experiences in two schools that approach either end of the spectrum. Barring this, student teaching should be done in situations that illustrate at least some of the better educational practices. To quote Mauritz Johnson (1962) again, "A situation does not have to be downright poor in order to be realistic'" (p. 58).

Since teachers holding either elementary or secondary certificates are permitted to teach in the junior high grades, both should be required to do at least some of their student teaching at this level. Otherwise, how can we claim any uniqueness for teaching in junior high? Moreover, a good junior high experience may attract into our ranks a number of teachers who, through prejudice or ignorance, have not previously given serious thought to teaching at this level.

The net result of the total recruitment, selection, and preparation process, regardless of the certificate, should be a teacher who has a broad general education, considerable depth in two or more teaching fields, sound professional preparation, and above all, commitment to teaching young adolescents. Commitment is one of the few significant differences we have found in comparing Cornell Project graduates with a group of equally inexperienced junior high teachers. At least more of them said they planned to continue teaching in junior high, and indicated, believe it or not, that they would reject an offer of a senior high position at comparable salary! What they actually do may be another matter.

Summary

In summary, this is what I have proposed:
1. Pre-service preparation of junior high teachers should differ in emphasis rather than kind from either elementary or secondary preparation.
2. The present practice of accepting either elementary or secondary certificates at the junior high level should be continued, provided that both programs include some student teaching at this level. The student teaching should be under the direction of a teacher committed to this level and in a school that exemplifies least some of the better contemporary practices.
3. A special junior high endorsement on either certificate should indicate completion of a program that includes:

  a. A broad general education
  b. Some depth in at least two teaching fields
  c. Some special attention to:
      (1) The nature of the young adolescents
      (2) The teaching of reading
      (3) The teacher's role in guidance and counseling
      (4) The history and philosophy of the junior high school.

Getting There from Here

If you accept these suggestions, how can we bring them about? First, we professors of education must provide a good junior high student teaching experience for all teachers whose certificates cover the junior high grades. This may mean a fight to win over our colleagues in the colleges of education, not to mention the state certification officials. Second, we must hold the line against efforts to stampede us into boosting subject field requirements for certificates so high as to rule out a teaching minor or a second teaching major. At the same time, we must encourage our colleagues in elementary education to consider giving elementary majors who seek a junior high endorsement some depth in at least two teaching fields. Finally, we in the colleges of education must offer prospective junior high teachers practical yet substantive courses or seminars in adolescent psychology, the teaching of reading, teacher-counseling, and junior high school education.

  Administrators have several key roles to play. First, they must aid college personnel in selecting really first-rate supervising teachers to guide practice teachers. At Cornell, we have learned from sad experience that even teachers nominated by junior high principals as "the best" in their schools, regardless of subject field, are not always effective either as teachers or as supervisors of beginners. Both college and public school staff should cooperate in selecting and training supervising teachers. Second, administrators bear the chief responsibility for making any junior high school a good place in which to teach and learn. Good teachers cannot be trained in poor schools; yet poor schools cannot be improved without good teachers. Here, again, cooperation of college, public school, and state education department staff is required. Continuous inservice development is especially important in junior high because of rapid teacher turnover.

Finally, administrators must remind themselves constantly that graduates of teacher preparation programs are not finished products. Beginners need special care during the first few years of teaching – decent teaching loads, adequate supervision, and lots of psychological support. One of our most creative and dynamic project interns was ready to quit teaching because she felt she had been tossed to the wolves by her administrator, who refused to back her in maintaining discipline or to give her any help in supervising a huge and rowdy study hall.

Junior high teachers and other staff members must join with administrators and college personnel to shape certification requirements so that future junior high teachers will have appropriate preparation. They also share responsibility for making every junior high program the best that can be achieved with the time, talent, and funds available. Too, they must be willing to tolerate diversity within their own ranks. The middle school in the educational system must continue to welcome both child-centered and subject-centered teachers, generalists as well as specialists, as long as they have the necessary commitment to teaching junior high youngsters.

All of us – professors, teachers, and administrators – must maintain the highest level of professionalism. The bitter disillusion some of our graduates feel when they face the "real world" is reflected in this portion of a letter written by a project intern after three months of full-time junior high teaching, announcing that she was leaving the profession:

> Whoever tries to defend the position that teaching is a profession might just as well give it up now. I've heard everything in teacher rooms from dirty jokes to "dirty niggers." There's no professional pride – it's just a job to them. And gossip about the kids is their second most favorite topic of conversation. As a sick footnote, one of

the married teachers has asked if he could see me some night when his wife goes out to her bridge game. (But of course any man could do that – it just rankles that he asked me in front of my class.)

Do you blame her for having second thoughts about teaching?

Each and every one of us must demonstrate by our own example the enthusiasm and dedication to teaching young adolescents that will lead students, other teachers, and the public at large to regard junior high teaching, not as a poor second choice for those who would rather do something else, but as the most rewarding and satisfying of careers. ▶

References

Beggs. III, D.W. (1964). Fundamental considerations for team teaching. In D.W. Beggs, III (Ed.), *Team teaching: Bold new venture* (p. 5). Indianapolis, IN: Unified College Press.

Briggs, T.H. (1920). *The junior high school.* Boston: Houghton Mifflin.

Hoots, Jr., W.R. (1963, October). Junior high school teacher certification. Bulletin of the *National Association of Secondary School Principals, 47*, 44-48.

Johnson. Jr., M. (1962, November). Preparation of teachers for the junior high school. *Teachers College Journal, 34*, 58.

Johnson, Jr., M. (1965). *A comparison between graduates of the Cornell Junior High School Project and other equally experienced junior high school teachers.* Ithaca, NY: Junior High School Project, Cornell University.

McGregor, A.L. (1929). *The junior high school teacher.* Garden City, NY: Doubleday, Doran.

New York State Education Department (n.d.). *Requirements for teaching in the elementary school.* Albany: NY: Author. (Mimeographed.)

New York State Education Department. (n.d.). *Amendment to Regulations of the Commissioner of Education Pursuant to Section 207 of the Education Law.* Albany: NY: Author.

Pabst, R.L. (1962). The junior high school teacher's certificate: Something new in teacher education. *Junior High School Newsletter, I* (1), 2-3.

Rice, A.H. (1964). What's wrong with junior highs? Nearly everything. *Nation's Schools, 74* (5), 32.

Shaplin, J. (1964). Toward a theoretical rationale for team teaching. In J.T. Shaplin & H.F. Olds (Eds.), *Team Teaching* (pp. 57-98). New York: Harper and Row.

Trump, J.L., & Baynham, D. (1961). *Focus on change: Guide to better schools*. Chicago: Rand McNally.

Wright, G.S., & Greer, E.S. (1963). *The junior high school: A survey of grades 7-8-9 in junior and junior-senior high schools*. Bulletin No. 32. U.S. Office of Education. Washington: DC: U.S. Government Printing Office.

Change – and the Junior High

Published in *Educational Leadership*, December 1965

*M*AN *the barricades! Here they come again!* These may
well be sentiments of elementary school educators as
they contemplate current changes in school organization. Having lost grades seven and eight to junior high school
"invaders" in a previous skirmish, not a few may feel they must
now muster their forces to save grades five and six from being
taken over by the new "middle school."

Imbedded in this conflict and permeating the consideration of all
issues in junior high school education today are fundamental
questions. These questions have been raised continually since
junior high schools began more than half a century ago: "Which
grade levels or ages should be included in the middle unit of the
school system?" "Should the middle unit be essentially a secondary school, an elementary school, or some peculiar blend of both?"
"What kind of educational program is best for young adolescents?"
"What kind of teacher is needed for this age?"

At present there is much talk and not a little action leading to
the establishment of the "middle school," a new intermediate unit
designed to replace junior high school and to embrace grades 6, 7,
and 8, or perhaps even grade 5 through 9. Elementary school
educators are not alone in fearing that this change may represent
merely another downward extension of secondary education,
without taking into account the special needs and characteristics
of the youngsters to be included in the newly constituted institution.

As long ago as 1894 the Committee of Ten on Secondary School
Studies suggested that secondary education begin in grade seven.
This trend was given added impetus by the highly influential
report of the Commission on the Reorganization of Secondary
Education, released in 1918. In addition to setting forth the famous

"Cardinal Principles of Secondary Education," the Commission stated:

> We...recommend a reorganization of the school system whereby the first six years shall be devoted to elementary education designed to meet the needs of pupils approximately 6 to 12 years of age; and the second six years to be secondary education designed to meet the needs of pupils approximately 12 to 18 years of age.

> The six years to be devoted to secondary education may well be divided into two periods which may be designated as the junior and senior periods. In the junior period emphasis should be placed upon the attempt to help the pupil explore his own aptitudes and make at least provisional choice of the kinds of work to which he shall devote himself. In the senior period emphasis should be given to training in the fields thus chosen. This distinction lies at the basis of the organization of the junior and senior high schools.

> In the junior high school there should be a gradual introduction of departmental instruction, some choice of subjects under guidance, promotion by subjects, prevocational courses, and a social organization that calls forth initiative and develops the sense of personal responsibility for the welfare of the group. (pp. 12-13)

Early advocates claimed that the new junior high school would offer "a program of studies decidedly greater in scope and richness of content than the traditional elementary school" (p. 7). Placing grades 7 and 8 in junior high would bring about "conditions for better teaching," and secure "better scholarship" (p. 18). To the extent that the "secondarization" of grades 7 and 8 has, in truth, resulted in more challenging subject matter, better qualified teachers, more adequate facilities, enriched student activities programs, etc., the change has benefited the students.

Intermediate institution

On the other hand, placing these grades in a "junior" secondary school led to the widely deplored tendency of some junior highs to ape the senior in unhealthy ways. Extreme specialization of subject matter has led in cases to an alienation of the junior high student from his teachers, a genuine loss in guidance at a time of life when he may need it most. Instruction may be highly formal and abstract, and college preparation unduly emphasized. In program, many junior high schools are indeed "vestibules molded in the architecture as the high schools to which they open" (p. 279).

Moreover, Dr. Conant's two-headed bête noire, interscholastic athletics marching bands, has flourished in some junior highs, not to mention formal dances and the precocious dating patterns that have alarmed many observers. Placing seventh and eighth graders in a junior high that is a mere carbon of an institution designed for older youth has often resulted in social activities, that are "too much, too soon." Little fifth and sixth graders must not be callously abandoned to such a fate, argue those who fear that the middle school may present yet another intrusion of secondary education patterns into the elementary school years.

Yet not all junior high schools have gone to the extremes indicated. To retain some features of the elementary school self-contained classroom, a large number of junior high schools have instituted block-time and core programs. Block-time is an antidote for extreme departmentalization, and it enables a teacher to know each student as a person, the first step toward effective guidance. Interdisciplinary team teaching programs, school-within-a-school organizations, and carefully developed homeroom guidance programs have all been used to make sure that the young junior high student is not "lost in the shuffle." Reading instruction, so crucial for academic success, is carried through grades seven, eight, and sometimes nine, either as a separate course or as part of an extended language arts or core period. A few junior high schools have even succeeded in de-emphasizing interscholastic sports and sophisticated social activities. In short, some junior high schools have retained some of the desirable features of the typical elementary school pattern. These junior high schools, not those that merely copy the senior high, may be considered the true prototypes of the emerging intermediate institution.

An institution that would truly serve the young adolescent in contemporary society will be neither elementary nor secondary in basic characteristics. It will combine the elementary school's traditional concern for the whole child with the secondary school's stress on scholarship and intellectual development. It will seek intellectual development through learning experiences in part organized around broad problems that are meaningful to students and in part through study in some depth of the recognized disciplines. It may provide this balance through some modification of the Dual Progress Plan, with an English-social studies core class for guidance and problem-centered learning paralleled by nongraded sequences taught by specialists in mathematics, science, art, and music.

Crucial to the success of such a combined approach is the development of middle school teachers whose preparation is neither exclusively secondary nor exclusively elementary in pattern, but a judicious blending of both, with special attention to teaching in the middle school.

Junior high schools are changing. Yet the basic question remains the same: "What shall be the nature of education for young adolescents in today's society?" Neither changing the institution's name nor moving its grade-level brackets up or down a notch will necessarily affect the character of the education it provides. Instead, educators at all levels must seize the opportunity represented by the present state of flux to try once again to make of the intermediate unit a truly unique institution for the age group it embraces. ❯

References

Alexander, W.M. (1965). The junior high school: A positive view. *Bulletin of the National Association of Secondary School Principals, 49* (299), 279.

Commission on the Reorganization of Secondary Education. (1918). *Cardinal principles of secondary education. Bulletin No. 35.* Washington, DC: Department of the Interior, Bureau of Education.

Davis, C.O. (1924). *Junior high school education.* Yonkers-on-Hudson, New York: World Book Company.

Koos, L.V. (1920). *The junior high school.* New York: Harcourt, Brace, and Howe.

National Educational Association. (1894). *Report of the Committee of Ten on secondary school studies.* New York: American Book Company.

Junior High or Middle School? Which Is Best for the Education of Young Adolescents ?

Adapted from remarks made at the Annual Conference of the Junior High
School Principals' Association of New York City, January 22, 1966

D ANTE SAID, "The hottest places in Hell are reserved for those who, in a period of moral crisis, maintain their neutrality." Controversy over whether the junior high or the middle school is the best organization for the education of young adolescents already has generated a good deal of heat. Those of us who try to maintain a neutral position may well find ourselves at the hottest point of the conflict. Nevertheless, doctrinaire advocacy of either form of school organization seems hardly warranted by the evidence presently available

But first, a prior question: Are there new goals for the education of young adolescents? I do not think so. The long-range goals of education for all our young people are still the same: (1) to develop citizens who can function effectively in our democratic society, and (2) to help each become a fully functioning individual. These are the educational goals of the entire society; many social agencies and institutions share responsibility for their attainment, including the home, the church, the schools, the mass media, and voluntary youth groups.

The special responsibility of the schools is intellectual development. It is their task to help each young person acquire the intellectual tools and concepts needed to become competent both as a citizen and as a person. Intellectual development in early adolescence is complicated by the stresses and strains imposed by our society on young people going through this period in life. Therefore, schools for this age must, in addition to intellectual development, give particular attention to guidance, exploration, and individualization, to cite three of the familiar functions of the junior high school. These goals and functions are appropriate for any institution composed primarily of young adolescents, whether it is called a junior high school, a middle school, a student center, or something else, or whether it contains grades 5-6-7-8, 6-7-8, 7-8-9, or no grades at all in some kind of nongraded program. In short, I believe that the goals of education for young adolescents are the same now as they were almost 60 years ago when the first junior high schools were organized.

Even if the goals have not changed, one may still ask whether there are educational and psychological bases for shifting from junior high school embracing grades 7 through 9 to a middle school embracing grades 6 through 8 or perhaps 5 through 8? (The two-year intermediate school is unacceptable to most educators because of the "revolving door effect" – students entering one year and leaving the next.) As far as the education of young adolescents is concerned, I believe it really does not matter whether they are in middle school or a junior high school – provided they have good teachers and a sound curriculum. Although good education can be provided under different organizational arrangements, the question is, will it? Is one arrangement more likely than another to attract qualified teachers? Does the pattern of grade organization materially affect the kind of curriculum and instruction provided? On these questions we have little evidence and much conjecture.

For example, William T. Gruhn (1966) asserts, on the basis of questionnaire studies of junior high school principals, that a 7-8-9 school is more likely to attract and retain competent guidance counselors and teachers who are well trained in subject matter. In addition, he feels that the junior high is more apt to attract men teachers than the middle school. This is mere opinion, but it is opinion that should be given serious consideration. If the presence of ninth graders in a school is, in truth, an inducement, then releasing the ninth grade to the high school may reduce the quality the teaching staff at the intermediate level. We need much more evidence before we can be sure this is the case, however.

The effect of school organization on curriculum is even more difficult to assess. In many junior high schools the ninth grade program is identical with that offered to freshmen in a conventional four-year high school. The curriculum is completely departmental-ized, ninth grade subjects "count" toward graduation, major and minor elective sequences are begun, and marks are reported on transcripts used for college admission. Without the ninth grade junior high school staff may feel less constrained to gear their program to the requirements of the high school. On the other hand, the middle school organization has been used in some places as a means of introducing departmentalization into grade levels formerly characterized by the self-contained classroom. I personally consider this a mistake, and am pleased to note that most of the middle schools studied by the NEA Research Division (1965) combine some departmentalization with some self-contained or block-time provisions, especially for grades 5 and 6. Thus a shift to the middle school may signal either an increase or a decrease in departmentalization of the curriculum, depending upon which approach school leaders consider more desirable for young adolescents.

Similar alternatives are evident with respect to ability grouping, electives, and other curriculum practices commonly associated with the high school, and with elementary school patterns such as the self-contained classroom. The middle school organization may provide an excuse for either downward extension of secondary education patterns or upward extension of elementary patterns. Neither is desirable, in my opinion. Instead, we should develop a curriculum specifically adapted to young people going through the in-between years, regardless of how the school is organized. This probably would combine some of the features now found in both elementary and secondary programs.

Most arguments concerning the junior high versus the middle school revolve around psychological factors. Here, too, the evidence is so tenuous that you can use it about any way you wish. Take the fact that youngsters nowadays reach puberty at a younger age and are more sophisticated and wise to the ways of the world than they used to be. This may be used to justify a 6-7-8 school on the grounds that sixth graders are ready for studies and social activities that are more advanced than those commonly provided in the elementary school. The same fact may be used to argue for a 7-8-9 pattern in order to keep youngsters in elementary school longer, thus hopefully protecting them from growing up too fast. We cannot answer the organizational question until we decide whether it is best to try to counteract the tendency toward early sophistication or to adjust our institutions to it.

Ambivalence also may be seen in our conception of what will happen to ninth graders if they are placed in high school. Some fear that they will begin steady dating earlier and imitate undesirable characteristics of the older adolescents; others assert that the older students, being more mature and stable, will be a good influence on them. Similar contradictory outcomes are predicted when sixth graders are placed in a middle school. In other words, older students may be viewed as either models or monsters. I am not aware of any conclusive evidence for either point of view; most students that I know combine a bit of both!

Alexander and Williams (1965) cite a study by Dacus suggesting on the basis of such factors as social, emotional, and physical maturity, plus opposite-sex choices, the least differences are found between students in grades six and seven, and between those in grades nine and ten. You will note that these are the very points where the breaks come when we have a 7-9 junior high school organization. Before we take this evidence too seriously, however, we need to know how the obvious differences in maturity of boys and girls were taken into account. In a similar study in upstate New York, Mauritz Johnson (1963) found that, in the judgment of teachers, sixth grade girls resembled seventh and eighth graders more than they did fifth graders, but ninth grade boys were more like seventh and eighth graders than they were like tenth graders. If we followed this lead, we would form our middle school of all seventh and eighth graders, plus sixth grade girls and ninth grade boys. Can you imagine trying to administer such an organizational monstrosity!

These are but a few of the claims and counterclaims favoring either the middle school or the junior high school. In some communities, political or sociological factors may weigh heavily, as the need to counteract the effects of de-facto segregation. In most cases, school organization decisions are based primarily on practical considerations – enrollment pressures and building facilities. On educational or psychological grounds, neither form organization can claim clear-cut advantages.

If this is the case, how should educators view a shift to a middle school organization? In the first place, let us recognize that the name "junior high school" has been an albatross around our necks from the beginning, and we are well rid of it. Operating under the middle school label, we may be able to resist the temptation to imitate the senior high. Perhaps we can get rid of inappropriate interscholastic sports and marching bands (if we ever had any) and can be sure that any social activities we sponsor are truly geared to the age group we serve. Perhaps we will no longer feel so much pressure to departmentalize the entire program; instead, we can expand our block-time and core programs since these can be, among other things, superior vehicles for providing the guidance our young people need. Without having to count ninth grade credits toward high school graduation, we may be more flexible in programming and utilizing nongraded, dual progress, and other individualized instruction approaches more extensively.

Any shake-up of an established pattern provides an excellent opportunity to make fundamental improvements. Whether we regard the change from the junior high to the middle school as a "revolution," a "reformation," or a "colossal mistake," let us seize this golden opportunity to make a fresh approach toward the goals we have always held for schools for young adolescents, however they are organized and whatever they are called. ❯

References

Alexander, W. & Williams, E. (1965). Schools for the middle school years. *Educational Leadership, 23* (3), 218.

Gruhn W. (1966, November 1). Remarks made at a meeting of the Lay Advisory Committee School District Reorganization, Ithaca, New York.

Johnson, Jr., M. (1963). *A pilot study of teachers' judgments of pupils' maturity in grades 6 through 9.* Ithaca, NY: Junior High School Project, Cornell University (Mimeographed).

National Education Association. (1965). Middle schools. *Educational Research Service Circular, No. 3.* Washington, DC: Author.

The Middle School:
Fresh Start or New Delusion?

Published in *The National Elementary Principal*,
November 1971. John H. Lounsbury co-author

AMERICANS worship the new, and educators are no exception. One "new" development in education that is attract-
ing a great deal of attention is the middle school, distin-
guished from the junior high school primarily by its inclusion of
younger children, usually grades 6 through 8 or even 5 through 8.
In their enthusiasm, some middle school advocates imply that this
reorganization will solve nearly all educational problems. It is time
to take a hardheaded look at the middle school movement and what
it really offers toward improving education.

The Problem of Levels

There is simply no satisfactory way to divide public education into
levels such as elementary and secondary. At their extremes, elementary and secondary are indeed relatively discrete levels, with both
real and implied differences in their objectives, approaches, and
programs. But where does elementary education end and secondary
begin?

Defensible decisions can only be made by considering each
individual child. Nancy, a well-developed and poised adolescent of
12, might successfully move into high school at the end of grade 7;
while George, small in size and social acumen, might better stay in
the elementary school until he reaches the middle of the ninth
grade at age 14. Presumably, such one-by-one placement could be
carried out under a nongraded or continuous progress arrangement.
Unfortunately, such programs are rare at the intermediate level, and
where they do exist, progress is usually determined by academic
performance, rather than social and emotional maturity.

In most school systems, the board of education must decide, more or less arbitrarily, which grades or ages will be placed in elementary schools and which in secondary. Inevitably, a decision to end elementary education after grade six is wrong for a large portion of the students affected, while another board's decision, to extend elementary education through grade eight is wrong for a different, but equally substantial, portion of the students.

Such difficulties are compounded rather than resolved when we introduce another school unit between elementary and secondary. Yet the need for some kind of intermediate unit for students going through their "in-between" years has been generally accepted for more than 50 years. There are, however, questions regarding what the intermediate unit should be called, what grades should be included, and what should be the fundamental nature of the program provided. Currently, these questions are being asked with increasing intensity.

Over the years, the original 8-4 division between elementary and secondary education all but passed out of the educational picture, replaced in most cases by the 6-3-3 plan elementary, junior high, senior high. At present, more than 8,000 separate junior high schools exist, with well over half of them having come into existence within the last 20 years. In some places, the junior high consists of grades 7 and 8, 6-7-8, or some other combination. However, the predominant pattern, generally preferred by educators and the public alike, has been the junior high school of grades 7 through 9.

Yet, just as the junior high school began to establish a virtual monopoly on intermediate education, a flood of questions concerning its success, its validity, and its appropriateness for the times began to be raised. The middle school was put forth as a better means of meeting the educational needs of early adolescents.

But what of the middle school? Is it unique? Different? More likely to succeed? And what of the junior high school? Has it failed? Is it outmoded? And where do elementary educators fit into this picture? These pertinent questions require careful consideration of the past, as well as present, trends and proposals.

The Junior High School Movement: A Review

In a complex, rapidly developing society such as ours, it is difficult, if not impossible, to isolate a movement and then analyze its causes and effects. So it is, and was, with the junior high movement. It was a broadly based movement, which gained supporters from many arenas of American life. It was influenced by both trends and countertrends.

Among early champions were psychologists such as G. Stanley Hall, whose theories concerning the adolescent years seemed to call for a special school with special treatment. College educators were especially prominent in the early reorganization movement, though often at odds with the psychologists. Public school educators supported the junior high as a means of "bridging the gap" between elementary and secondary programs and hoped through the earlier introduction of vocational education to make schooling more relevant to daily life. Civic and government leaders who were interested in the adequate "Americanization" of immigrants saw the junior high school as a possible solution for this societal problem. Taxpayers, vexed over the excessive cost of educating large numbers of repeating students, found in the proposed intermediate school a possible means of saving funds.

Although first advocated as a downward extension of secondary education, the junior high came more and more to be justified, at least in theory, on the basis of meeting the needs of the young adolescent. This point of view parallels the concern for the whole child," common among elementary educators.

Often, expedient administrative factors were major, if not sole, reasons for establishing junior high schools. In the years following World War I, there was a tremendous need for new school buildings to relieve overcrowding, and the creation of a new intermediate unit often seemed to be the most economical solution at hand. So, with many divergent supporters and a lot of assistance from timing and administrative realities, the junior high grew and grew. But did it really succeed? The answer is both yes and no.

The junior high school has served rather well as a pilot school for educational innovations, such as core curriculum and team teaching. Less burdened with precedent and tradition, this new school unit has been quite experimental. Yet it has failed to implement broadly the full aspirations of its supporters. This is hardly surprising in view of the fantastic claims made by some junior high advocates. There is remarkably little exaggeration in Johnson's (1964) statement:

> They proposed to develop healthy individuals of sound moral character who were guaranteed not only to be competent in their jobs and wise in their use of leisure, but worthy parents and good citizens to boot. Indeed, some assurance was offered that in the process the pupil might also enjoy popularity among his peers, a tranquil adolescence, and protection from a sense of failure and frustration. (p. 122)

The junior high school has enjoyed tremendous success in terms of administrative organization. As early as 1930, nearly half of all secondary pupils were attending reorganized schools. Today, we estimate that nearly 80 percent of America's pupils go through some form of intermediate school.

In this numerical success, the junior high school is so like America generally. As a people, we have been "quantity" successful beyond all anticipation; yet a "quality" success continues to elude us – in democratic government, social and human relationships, religion, business enterprises, and the like. We have organizational and technological answers in abundance, but often they do not solve the fundamental human problems.

Now the junior high school is under attack, primarily on the grounds that it has modeled itself too closely on the senior high school. Interscholastic athletics, marching bands, and sophisticated social activities have moved with little modification into the junior high, to the dismay of many educators and parents. Instruction is too often formal and discipline centered, with insufficient attention given to the student as a person. (Ironically, the very specialization of instruction that is criticized in the junior high has been put forth as an argument for the middle school, which is expected to bring the benefits of specialized teaching to younger students.) In short, the junior high is charged with failure to provide a program, both academic and social, that is geared to the needs and characteristics of the emerging adolescent.

Perhaps its age also makes the junior high vulnerable to attack at this particular point in history. Although really still young, it has nevertheless been around long enough – 60 years – to be identified with the status quo, the establishment, and yet not long enough to have accumulated the support of tradition, as have the elementary school and the high school.

The Middle School Movement: A Perspective

Looking at the junior high and middle school movements with a historical perspective, one can see the cyclical nature of social change. The junior high school cycle could aptly be characterized as moving from one Harvard president to another: that is, from Charles W. Eliot's earliest advocacy of reorganization in 1888 through James B. Conant's junior high school report in 1960. In that first cycle, the school started with a college-dominated concern for academic efficiency, with shortening the length of elementary education and introducing high school subjects earlier. Later, the junior high school became an instrument of the progressive era. Concern with individuality, creativity, student needs, and personal values was reflected in the widespread acceptance of the core curriculum, for example. In the late 1950s, the cycle shifted back toward academic emphases as the post-sputnik obsession with intellectual development swept the land.

The middle school cycle began in the 1960s as the discipline-centered national curriculum projects were bringing "new" mathematics, "new" science, "new" social studies, "new" English, and other programs into the schools. Intellectual concerns led some intermediate schools to cast off the ninth grade so that it could be reattached to the senior high, where, presumably, more effective sequences in the sciences, mathematics, and foreign languages might be developed. Adding fifth and sixth grades to the middle unit was advocated to bring students the benefits of instruction by more specialized teachers, a further downward extension of the secondary pattern of curriculum organization.

Already this portion of the cycle is passing as schools, responding in part to the criticisms of the "new romantics" like Holt and Goodman, seek once again to humanize education in what may be characterized as a rebirth of progressive education. Core curriculum is being rediscovered or reinvented, often under such labels as "humanities" or the "open curriculum."

Only the passage of time will reveal how much further the middle school will retrace the junior high cycle. But it seems certain that it will be no less influenced by the varied realities of school size, pupil population, and existing buildings than was the junior high school before it. The middle school is hardly immune to the same viruses that handicapped the full development of the junior high school. One need not be surprised, then, if a middle school somewhere organizes a marching band, fields a varsity football team, conducts formal graduation exercises, or otherwise follows the American secondary pattern, thus illustrating the well-known gap between theory and practice.

Placing the middle school movement in this historical perspective is not intended to suggest fatalistic resignation or hopelessness. Rather, it is to provide perspective from which to view contemporary educational programs, proposals, and possibilities. As Santayana warned, "Those who cannot remember the past are condemned to repeat it."

It will be many years before a definitive history of the middle school movement can be written. Intermediate schools that encompass the grades or age levels now advocated for the middle school have been in existence since the very early days of the junior high. The term middle school has been applied to some intermediate units for more than 40 years, often in private schools modeled on the European pattern. Yet, since the mid-1960s, the number of middle schools has increased rapidly. Although researchers have used slightly different definitions and sampling techniques, it appears that the number grew from approximately 500 in 1965-66 (Cuff, 1967) to more than 1,000 in 1967-68 (Alexander, 1969) to at least 1,300 in 1969-70 (Mellinger & Rackauskas, 1970). It should be recognized that this growth has not been entirely at the expense of existing junior high schools. Many new junior highs have been organized during this same period.

It is unclear at present how many districts merely changed the name of an existing school, how many regrouped grade levels without making any substantial changes in program, and how many made a sincere effort to build a new educational program from the ground up. Thus far, surveys reveal very few significant differences between junior highs and middle schools (Gatewood, 1971; Mellinger & Rackauskas, 1970).

Unfortunately, reorganization has been accompanied by a great deal of educational "bandwagoning," with advocacy of overly simplistic organizational answers to tough educational problems and shortsighted failure to recognize the almost complete overlap of concerns and proposals between junior high advocates and middle school champions.

Arguments for the Middle School

What do educators hope to accomplish by reorganizing the school system to provide for a middle school? The arguments are diverse and sometimes, as in the junior high movement, seemingly contradictory. Often, the case rests on overcoming the weaknesses of the junior high school or in simply doing better what the junior high is already attempting, such as easing the students' transition from elementary to high school or providing a program especially designed for the age group. Other arguments, some already alluded to, require fuller examination if the middle school movement is to be given the thoughtful analysis it deserves.

Precocity of the learner. Much has been made of the purported earlier maturation of young people today. Not only do they reach puberty at an earlier age, 16, but they are more sophisticated and wise in the ways of the world, largely as a result of television and other mass media. It is argued that fifth and sixth graders are therefore ready for the greater academic and social challenges offered in a middle school .

In opposition, it is pointed out that earlier biological maturation has not been adequately documented and that, regardless, it does not necessarily bring with it the intellectual, social, and psychological maturity necessary to handle most middle school programs. According to this view, middle schools are accused of aiding and abetting a questionable tendency toward early sophistication that is robbing children of their childhood. Educators might better keep children in the elementary school longer in order to shield them from excessive academic pressure and the possible harmful influence of older youth.

Segregation of the emerging adolescent. Both junior highs and middle schools have been viewed as sanctuaries in which youngsters can work out the problems associated with puberty without the distractive presence of other age groups, especially older adolescents. Whether older youth represent a harmful or helpful influence is highly debatable, of course. It is ironic that some middle school advocates would remove ninth graders from the intermediate unit to protect seventh and eighth graders, giving little thought to what may happen to immature ninth graders as they try to adjust to a large, complex, impersonal high school. These advocates may then turn around and place fifth or sixth graders in the same school with eighth graders, who are viewed by many teachers as the wildest bunch of all!

Homogeneity of the age group. Middle school proponents have gone to considerable lengths to demonstrate that sixth and seventh graders are more alike than are eighth and ninth graders in terms of social and emotional maturity. Such arguments are specious at best, for they overlook large sex differences. Johnson (1963) explored this issue in a pilot study in which 124 teachers in eight schools rated 3,583 students on whether they most resemble students in the grades above them or below them in social-emotional maturity. If one were to implement the results of this study, the intermediate unit would consist of sixth grade girls, seventh and eighth grade boys and girls, and ninth grade boys. One wonders how many communities are ready for this kind of organization

Moreover, maturation is a-phasic; that is, social maturation is not necessarily in step with physical maturation or social maturation, so it is difficult to see how any general index of maturity could be developed and applied. Add the rapidity with which changes are taking place along each of these lines during the school year, and you have a tremendously complicated situation.

Reorganization arguments based on homogeneity also fail to take into account a basic concept that is fundamental to any intermediate school. Whatever its name or grade level organization, it exists to help young people make the transition from childhood to adulthood. The elementary school is for children. The high school is for adolescents. The middle unit is for those in between, for those in transition from one stage to another. The grade grouping is not designed to bring together like pupils but rather to bring together diverse pupils, pupils whose common characteristic is their unlikeness, not their likeness. In short, no intermediate grade grouping, 6-8 any more than 7-9, is defensible from the standpoint of the general homogeneity of the pupils concerned.

Curricular autonomy. It has been said that the ninth grade inhabits the junior high "for rations and quarters only," since its program is often dictated almost entirely by the high school. Carnegie Units, graduation credits and transcripts, not to mention "freshman" football and junior varsity basketball, all give evidence of how the ninth grade may be tied to the high school. Presumably, a middle school without grade nine would be free to develop a program without these restraints.

However, one need not amputate the ninth grade to develop programs suitable for young adolescents. Wherever the ninth grade is housed, its program must still articulate with the grades above and below. Ninth grade credits do not have to be counted toward graduation, as many junior high schools can demonstrate, and a senior high can still win football or basketball games even without a farm team in the junior high. Where junior high schools have yielded to high school dictation, it is more often the fault of leadership than the pattern of organization. In other words, strong, independent programs, suited to the needs of the age group, can and have been developed in many intermediate schools, with or without the ninth grade.

Specialized instruction The opportunity to provide instruction by subject matter specialists was one of the early arguments for the junior high school, and it is once again prominent in the rationale for the middle school. It is not an unmixed blessing, as evidenced by the frequency with which this very feature is the target of attacks on the junior high today. In any intermediate school, specialization must be counterbalanced by deliberate efforts to help students to see life as a whole, to fit the pieces together in some meaningful way. This is one reason why core curriculum, block-time programs, and interdisciplinary team teaching have long been prominent in both junior highs and middle schools.

Individualization, flexibility, and innovation. Individual differences among students reach their peak during adolescence. In the past, educators have responded with such approaches as ability grouping, projects, committee work, promotion by subject, elective courses, and student activities. Now we have more sophisticated procedures, such as nongraded programs, individually prescribed instruction, independent study, and programed instruction.

Individualization can be carried too far, of course, and this can be especially damaging at a time of life when peer relationships are so important to a youngster. A sound program for this age provides for both individual study and ample opportunity to work with others.

If middle schools seem to have gone further toward individualized instruction than some of the older junior highs, no doubt an important factor is the educational climate in which they came into being. The same can be said for flexible scheduling, team teaching, the open school plan, and other innovations. Planning a new building is an especially propitious opportunity to introduce new ideas, whether it be an elementary, middle, junior high, or high school. To justify the middle school as a means of introducing innovations, as some have done, is to miss the point entirely.

Guidance. It has long been recognized that a young person during his transition years especially needs the advice and guidance of an adult who knows him well and cares about him as a person. Teachers can fulfill this role in a carefully developed core, block-time, home base, or advisement team program. There appears to be no particular reason why this would be any easier in a middle school than in a junior high, given the proper staff and leadership.

Some educators justify returning the ninth grade to the high school to give guidance counselors one more year to become acquainted with a student before they have to make recommendations for college, employment, military service, and the like. Too often, however, this gain is accompanied by a sacrifice in the kind of personal guidance more often found in the junior high or middle school, so there may be a net loss of guidance to the ninth graders.

Staff. As we have seen, some of the ills of the junior high are attributed to the fact that they are staffed primarily with secondary teachers, presumably rather narrowly trained and concerned mainly with subject matter. The middle school might give young people in their transition years more opportunity to interact with elementary-trained staff members, welcomed because of their broader training, their familiarity with the teaching of reading, and their supposedly child-centered point of view.

In many states, however, teachers with elementary certification have always been able to teach in junior high schools, at least through grade eight. Moreover, the opportunity to work with ninth graders has held some of our better teachers and counselors in the junior high. There is some concern that, with the removal of the ninth grade, the middle school will lose some of its best staff members to the high school. There is also the fear that, since male teachers tend to prefer the upper grades, middle schools will have fewer male teachers, and elementary schools almost none.

Administrator certification is another problem. In states where junior high principals must have secondary certification, they must either move on or seek recertification as elementary principals if their schools drop the ninth grade.

For various reasons, colleges and universities have never prepared many teachers specifically for the intermediate level. The advent of the middle school may pose even greater problems, especially for elementary educators.

One difficulty results from the development of early childhood education programs. These are concerned with what we have mistakenly labeled preschool, plus the first three grades. As middle schools move down to include grade six and sometimes grade five, early childhood specialists are beginning to assume responsibility for the primary grades, leaving general elementary education with sole responsibility for only the fourth grade! The head of elementary education in one university has been labeled (jokingly?) by his colleagues as "chairman of the fourth grade," since his university has a special middle school program (grades 5-8) and an ongoing early childhood education program (nursery-grade 3). Now along come Mellinger and Rackauskas (1970), recommending that grade four be included in the middle school! Just how many levels of education can be justified in terms of distinctive programs, specially trained personnel, and special facilities?

Perhaps more widespread adoption of continuous progress or nongraded programs, coupled with the much-debated single certificate, will eliminate these issues before they become too acute. However, we predict considerable controversy as elementary educators deal with what they may well consider to be attacks from both above and below. The middle school-junior high school issue cannot be settled apart from these related problems.

School desegregation. The middle school has been viewed by some minority groups as a means of getting children out of segregated neighborhoods earlier – in grades 5 or 6, rather than 7 or 8. While recognizing the validity of this objective, segregation is too complex a problem to be solved by such a process, and we may well question whether it is fair to the children to use the schools for this purpose. The current school busing controversy illustrates the difficulties that arise when we try to use the schools to solve grave sociopolitical problems.

Buildings and finances It is a perennial complaint that many junior high schools have had to subsist on leftovers – buildings abandoned by an elementary or high school, staff members marking time until retirement or waiting for a high school opening, elementary principals who have grown weary of dealing with younger children, or high school teachers seeking administrative positions but who are not quite good enough for a high school post. It remains to be seen whether the middle school will suffer a similar fate. Board members and school administrators must see that children at all levels get their fair share of the best facilities and materials obtainable with available funds.

After all is said and done, most school reorganizations take place because of enrollment pressures, building needs, or budgetary problems; in other words, for reasons that are more administrative than educational (Gatewood, 1971). This has been true of the junior high, and it is equally true of the middle school. Many fine new institutions, carefully planned from curriculum to staff to building, have resulted from enrollment pressures, and one can sympathize with the school board that, in times of austerity, decides to build a middle school rather than a junior high in order to save the cost of some special facilities and equipment.

What is distressing, however, is that some educators hide these real reasons under a smoke screen of rhetoric about the educational, social, or psychological advantages of a middle school, arguments that simply do not hold up under analysis, as can be seen from the preceding paragraphs. It is far better to admit that exigencies require a reorganization and then to enlist the energies of staff, students, parents, and the community to take fullest possible advantage of the opportunity for a fresh start.

Sometimes it seems easier to tear down an old building and build a new one than to renovate an existing structure. Perhaps it is necessary to tear down the junior high school in order to bring about an intermediate institution more closely attuned to the times and to the young people it serves. In doing so, however, let us not delude ourselves and the public that the new structure will automatically usher in the millennium. Just as it is the people and their quality of living that make a house a home, so the staff and the curriculum are what really make the school. If the junior high school has failed, it is because its reach exceeded its grasp. Let us not make the same mistake with the middle school. Let us, rather, set modest, realistic goals, evaluate our work carefully and be frank in reporting both successes and failures.

The appearance of the middle school should be viewed, not as a new answer, a new solution, but as a new opportunity, a new rallying point, a fresh start. The goals of the middle school and the junior high school are the same. The educational tools and techniques available to achieve these goals are the same; the vehicles in which we travel are almost the same; and the roadblocks to be removed or skirted confront all who travel this way. The road to improved educational experiences for young adolescents is a difficult one – history certainly teaches us that – but we are all on the same road. All concerned must work together to provide vital and appropriate educational experiences for youth in the critical transitional years. ▶

References

Cuff, W.A. (1967). Middle schools on the march. *Bulletin of the National Association of Secondary School Principals. 51*, 84.

Gatewood, T.E. (1971). *What research says about the junior high versus the middle school.* Paper presented at the 1971 Annual Meeting of the North Central Association, Chicago. (Mimeographed).

Johnson, M., Jr. (1963). *A pilot study of teachers' judgments of pupils' maturity in grades 6 through 9.* Ithaca, NY: Junior High School Project, Cornell University (Mimeographed).

Johnson, M., Jr. (1964). The dynamic junior high school. *Bulletin of the National Association of .Secondary School Principals 48,* 122.

Mellinger, M., & Rackauskas, J. (1970). *Quest for identity: National survey of the middle school, 1969-70.* Chicago: Chicago State College.

Moss, T.C. (1969). The middle school comes – and takes another grade or two. *National Elementary Principal 48,* 37-41.

Post, R.L. (1968). Middle school: A questionable innovation. *Clearing House 42,* 484-86.

Sanders, S.G. (1968). Challenge of the middle school. *Educational Forum 32,* 191-97.

Van Til, W., Vars, G.F., & Lounsbury, J.H. (1967). *Modern education for the junior high school years* (2nd ed.). Indianapolis, IN: Bobbs-Merril.

Vars, G.F. (1966). Junior high or middle school? Which Is best for the education of young adolescents? *High School Journal, 50,* 109-13.

Vars, G. F. (1969). Teacher preparation for the middle schools. *High School Journal, 53,* 172-177.

Vars, G.F., (Ed.). (1969). Common learnings: Core and interdisciplinary team approaches. Scranton, PA: International Textbook Company

Gordon F. Vars reflects...

"You've come a long way, Baby!"

Y es, the middle school movement has come a long way, and it has been my good fortune to have been involved in it from the very beginning. In July, 1963, I was present when William M. Alexander addressed the topic "The Junior High: A Changing View" at Cornell University's Tenth Annual Conference for School Administrators. There had been talk about reorganizing the junior high school for some time, but Dr. Alexander's eloquently articulated vision and tireless efforts to promote the idea rightfully earned him the title of "Father of the Middle School" (Alexander & George, 1981, 1993).

But in a sense, the middle school is not really a newborn. Rather, it is a reincarnation of the junior high school ideal advanced since the turn of the century by far-sighted educators like T. H. Briggs, Leonard V. Koos, William Smith, Aubrey A. Douglass, William T. Gruhn, and Harl R. Douglass. While their proposals varied, they all saw the need for an educational institution geared specifically to the unique characteristics and needs of young people making the transition from childhood to adolescence. The middle school was intended to make this kind of education available to younger students, who were reaching puberty earlier and seemed to be growing up faster than earlier generations.

Unfortunately, not all the middle school "baby's" movements have been forward. It is true that middle level schools encompass-ing grades 5-8 or 6-8 (usually called "middle schools") now out-number schools enrolling grades 7-9 (usually called "junior high schools"). But the educational experiences offered within these reorganized schools still look a lot like those found in the junior high schools of the 1930s and 40s. When in 1966 Neal C. Nickerson, Jr., wrote *Junior High Schools Are on the Way Out*, he underestimated the tenacity with which educators would retain traditional practices regardless of what grade levels are housed together or what the middle level institution is called.

One way to examine how far we have come and how far we still have to go is to look again at the philosophical framework of the junior high school. For decades, junior high school educators have been guided by the "functions of the junior high school" first identified by William T. Gruhn in 1940. Functions were defined as "those conditions or elements in the program of the junior high school which will lead most directly to the fullest realization of the ultimate aims of education" (Gruhn & Douglass, 1971, p. 72). Gruhn focused on functions of special importance to schools serving young people of junior high or middle school age: Integration, Exploration, Guidance, Differentiation, Socialization, and Articulation.

These functions were elaborated in three editions of *The Modern Junior High School,* a highly influential book that Gruhn wrote with his mentor, Harl R. Douglass (1947, 1956, 1971). These functions also were evident in one form or another in major books on middle school education published during the first two decades of the current movement (Vars, 1984). They live on today, at least in spirit, in such statements as the Carnegie Council on Adolescent Development's *Turning Points* (1989) and the National Middle School Association's *This We Believe: Developmentally Responsive Middle Level Schools* (1995).

Integration

By integration, Gruhn and Douglass meant that student learnings should be integrated or incorporated into "effective and wholesome behavior," not merely memorized long enough to pass a test. To accomplish this, all students were to be provided "a broad, general, common education in the basic knowledges and skills." The total program was to be made coherent through "effective correlation among the studies, learning activities, and extraclass activities."

To fulfill this function, block-time and core programs were widely adopted by junior high schools. These curriculum designs had been pioneered by the secondary schools involved in the famous Eight Year Study of the Progressive Education Association (Aikin, 1942;

Lipka, Lounsbury, Toepfer, Vars, Alessi, & Kridel, 1998). In these programs, one teacher teaches two or more different subjects to the same group of students during an extended period of time, hence the term "block- time." Core is a special variation of this approach in which the curriculum is focused directly on the needs, interests, and concerns of students, and they are directly involved in planning their own learning experiences. Several surveys carried out in the 1940s and 50s found block-time or core programs in about half the nation's junior high schools. (See Wright and Greer, 1963.)

In contrast, middle schools, following the lead of William Alexander, Paul George, and others, opted for the interdisciplinary team organization. While these teams reduce teacher isolation and break up large schools into smaller learning communities, they often get in the way of curriculum integration. Whereas a block-time teacher can work out curriculum connections by him/her self, in a team these must be negotiated with several different personalities, each of whom usually represents a different subject area. When interdisciplinary teams work well, they are a joy to behold, but too often students merely rotate among the teachers on the team, with little curricular connection. Thus some middle school programs are even more departmentalized than the junior high schools they replaced.

There has been a remarkable resurgence of interest in curriculum integration during the 1990s. This is evident from the many publications, workshops, and conference presentations advocating that approach and describing successful programs (See, for example: Beane, 1993; Stevenson & Carr, 1993; NMSA, 1995). Yet when actual classroom instruction is examined closely, little curriculum integration may be evident, even in schools with well-established interdisciplinary teams (Lounsbury and Clark, 1990).

Too often, the mechanics of coordinating the efforts of four to six teachers leaves little time to plan integrative curriculum. In response, some schools are rediscovering the benefits of small two-person or "partner" teams (Alexander, Carr, & McAvoy, 1995; Arnold & Stevenson, 1998). In this arrangement, only two or three teachers work with the same group of students. Each may be responsible for instruction in more than one subject, as in a block-time class. This approach to teaming was advocated years ago by Bair and Woodward (1964) as being especially appropriate for elementary schools. Perhaps the next step is to re-discover the values of the "solo" block-time teacher or self-contained class!

Of course, teachers must have appropriate preparation and certification to teach combined subjects. The broad preparation provided for most elementary teachers fits them well for this approach, and since 1991 the National Middle School Association's *NCATE - Approved Curriculum Guidelines* has recommended that middle level teachers be prepared in two teaching fields. However, special certification for teaching at the middle level is mandated in very few states, and colleges and universities have been slow to offer programs for this level.

Without strong preservice or inservice staff development, integration, a function of the middle level school advocated since the 1940s by Gruhn and Douglass, is not likely to become widespread in middle level schools, whatever they are called.

Guidance

In addition to integration, junior high block-time and core teachers were expected to carry out the guidance function, absorbing many of the tasks of the traditional homeroom. Working with the same students for several periods every day, these teachers become very well acquainted with a relatively small number of students. Block-time programs that approach the core ideal also incorporate guidance content directly into the curriculum. Teacher-student-planned units deal with such student concerns as self-understanding, getting along with others, or planning for the future. Knowing students as persons and dealing directly with their daily concerns enable the teacher to help students "make intelligent decisions" concerning their future education and vocations, two critical elements of the guidance function as described by Gruhn and Douglass. With appropriate support from guidance specialists, block-time teachers also help students to grow "toward wholesome, well-adjusted personalities" and to "reach the fullest development of their individual interests and talents."

In many middle schools, this teacher-guidance function is carried out in an advisory program in which a teacher assumes personal responsibility for "getting close" to 12 to 15 students. While many of these programs work very well, in too many cases teachers see this as just one more task added to an already-impossible teaching load. Moreover, in order to form such small student groups, nearly every staff member of the school must be assigned a group. This virtually guarantees that at least some of the advisors will be less than enthusiastic about assuming this role.

As an alternative, some middle schools make student guidance one of the tasks of interdisciplinary teams. This may place the entire responsibility on only a few faculty, usually those who teach the so-called academic subjects. It also may deny students the opportunity to be in advisory groups with teachers of exploratory classes or support staff like the media specialist. Moreover, unless teams are given additional time and assistance with this function, guidance is likely to be overlooked in the day-by-day press of other responsibilities.

The relative merits of providing guidance through advisory programs, block-time, or other approaches have been described elsewhere (Vars, 1989; 1997). Schools that take the student guidance function seriously might best consider combining a variety of approaches. But without firm commitment by the entire staff, the guidance function identified years ago by Gruhn and Douglass may continue to be slighted in many middle level schools.

Exploration

To Gruhn and Douglass, exploration had both a personal and a societal justification. The junior high school was expected to "lead students to discover and explore their specialized interests, aptitudes, and abilities as a basis for decisions regarding educational opportunities" and for "present and future vocational decisions." It was assumed that individuals would be more successful in life if they were helped to make wise decisions in those areas. In addition, society would be a better place if students developed "a continually widening range of cultural, social, civic, avocational, and recreational interests."

Gruhn and Douglass argued that exploration was a responsibility of the total school program, but in many junior high schools it was relegated largely to required courses in art, music, industrial arts, and home economics, supplemented by a number of "extracurricular" clubs and activities. This pattern was adopted by most middle schools. In fact, the "exploratory wheel," in which students rotate among six- or nine-week courses, still is a common pattern. The distinctions between "academic" and "exploratory" courses sometimes leads to perceived differences in teacher's status. This is aggravated by schedules that provide common planning time for interdisciplinary academic teams while their students are in exploratory classes, without giving exploratory teachers similar planning opportunities. As some bitter exploratory teachers put it, "We baby-sit their kids while they do their planning!"

The rise of unionism in education and current budget problems also have taken their toll of the important exploratory function in middle level schools. Student club and activity programs, either within school hours or afterwards, are viewed by many teachers as one more uncompensated class preparation, so they are reluctant to get involved. And the strong pressure for academic achievement as measured by state proficiency tests keeps many teachers from making their regular courses truly exploratory. Compton and Hawn in 1993 and the NMSA in its 1995 position paper have renewed the call to make the entire middle level curriculum exploratory, but it is too soon to see how schools will respond.

In short, exploration is a function that has been imperfectly carried out throughout the history of middle level education, and the prospects for improvement are unclear at this time.

Differentiation

Many middle schools seem to be doing much better on the function of differentiation than their junior high predecessors. To Gruhn and Douglass, this function meant that a school should provide "differentiated educational facilities and opportunities suited to the varying backgrounds, interests, aptitudes, abilities, personalities, and needs of students." This required "learning activities in all areas of the educational program which will be challenging, satisfying, and at a level of achievement appropriate to students of different backgrounds, interests, abilities, and needs."

In junior high schools, the differentiation function was largely accomplished by tracking and ability grouping, although small group work and independent study were provided in many classes, especially in block-time programs. Students unable to function in even the lower tracks were served in special education programs, often in segregated facilities and sometimes in separate schools. Similarly, gifted and talented students were segregated and served in special sections, pull-out classes, extracurricular programs, or even special schools.

Middle schools today have access to wide variety of technological tools for differentiation instruction, such as interactive computer programs, CD ROMs, and the nearly infinite resources of the world-wide web. They also can capitalize on recent research that identifies additional ways in which individuals differ, such as learning styles, multiple intelligences, and left-right brain preferences. Moreover, teachers today have at their disposal more research and experience with cooperative learning procedures that challenge individual students within a heterogeneous class (Tomlinson, 1995). Of course, in most schools, large class sizes and heavy teaching loads make it difficult for teachers to carry out procedures that they know could better provide for individual differences among their students.

Modern-day middle schools also are in the vanguard of efforts to "detrack" schools, and "full inclusion" of both "challenged" and "gifted" students is found in more and more schools. Neither of these changes has gone smoothly, however, and too often educational leaders underestimate the time and effort needed to build programs that adequately differentiate instruction (Wheelock, 1992).

Improvement in this aspect of education also is hampered by the all-too-human tendency to think in either-or terms; a school is expected to be either fully tracked or completely heterogeneous. Instead, a balance of mostly heterogeneous classes combined with carefully-planned special programs and activities might be most appropriate (Vars & Rakow, 1993).

To summarize, we know a lot more today about how individuals differ, and middle school teachers have a much larger array of tools with which to provide differentiated instruction. However, logistical constraints still keep many schools and teachers from using these resources effectively.

Socialization

Socialization is the term Gruhn and Douglass applied to both preparation for effective citizenship in our society and for "participation in an effective and mature manner in the activities of young adolescents and, later, as older adolescents and adults." At one time, "civics" was taught directly in many junior high schools, and student government was expected to served as a proving ground for democratic ideals and practices. School dances and parties, field trips, outdoor education, drama and music performances, sports and intramurals all were expected to help young people learn to work harmoniously with others.

Unfortunately, social activities in too many junior high schools imitated the senior high, including activities like proms, crowning homecoming kings and queens, fraternities and sororities, and other activities not suitable for most young adolescents. Middle schools, since they included students even younger than the typical junior high, have to be especially vigilant. Young people's eagerness to take on grown-up ways may push schools into providing activities and programs more suitable for older teens while neglecting those more age-appropriate.

Sports provide a prime example of this pressure. Some middle schools, again driven by either-or thinking, tried to abolish all interscholastic sports in favor of intramurals. They quite properly cited the statistics on sports injuries in young people who are still going through puberty. They pointed out how overemphasis on athletics and the varsity "cut" system hurt many young people, including those who in a few years might become star athletes. Some middle schools, on the other hand, have both a strong intramural program and a no-cut policy for both sports teams and cheerleaders. But they also recognize the need to provide some limited and carefully-supervised opportunities for physically mature boys and girls to compete with other schools. In a sense they have re-invented the "play days" and "extra-mural" activities pioneered by early junior high schools. Here, again, wise application of "both-and" serves young people better than "either-or."

With more students coming to school from dysfunctional families and less-than-desirable neighborhoods, schools today are expected to provide students with even more help in learning social skills, concepts, and values. This expectation often seems to conflict with demands for greater academic rigor and with ever-present budget constraints. As a result, socialization still receives little direct attention as a vital function of the school, even in more affluent districts.

Articulation

The articulation function is imposed on middle level schools by their position between elementary schools and high schools. Gruhn and Douglass called for programs and policies to provide for a "gradual transition" from one institutional level to the next. The need remains the same, whether the middle level includes grades 5-8, 7-9, or some other combination.

Block-time programs were promoted in junior high schools as representing a gradual transition from the self-contained elementary classroom to the full departmentalization of the high school. Similar arguments are sometimes used today for interdisciplinary teaming, although the widespread use of teams in elementary schools tends to undercut that argument. Middle school advisory programs also are expected to help young people adjust to the new building, which often is much larger and more complex than their neighborhood elementary school.

In any case, young people slated to move into a different building for their middle level education need to be "oriented" to the new institution. This usually involves sending teachers, counselors, administrators, and sometimes students into the elementary schools to describe what is ahead and to answer questions. Elementary students also may visit the middle level school to begin getting used to it. The younger children coming into middle schools today require even greater care than did the seventh graders moving to the junior high. Simmons and Blyth (1987) have documented the often-traumatic effects of this transition on young people, but their recommendations have not yet received the attention they deserve.

Smoothing the transition from the middle level to the high school has proved more problematical. High schools too often make no special provisions for incoming students, except to send high school counselors to the middle level school to enroll students in courses. Fortunately, some schools are now establishing special ninth-grade houses or teams to provide for both the academic and emotional needs of newcomers to the building. Still too rare are programs like that described by Ross Burkhardt of Shoreham-Wading River Middle School in New York, in which teachers help graduating middle school students "learn to say farewell" (1985).

In terms of curriculum, articulation of content and skills across the K-12 continuum still is haphazard at best, and it is the rare school system that enables elementary, middle, and high school teachers to meet on a regular basis to coordinate programs and activities.

In short, articulation is a function that both junior highs and middle schools are apt to address primarily for students coming into the school, not those exiting, and curriculum articulation receives too little attention in any kind of middle level school.

Conclusion

This brief review of developments in middle level education over the past few decades reveals some important gains, and also much room for improvement. There is no doubt that the middle school *movement* is going strong, at least in terms of grade level configuration. Having helped to launch its predecessor organization, the Midwest Middle School Association, I have watched with a great deal of satisfaction the phenomenal growth of the National Middle School Association. State and regional associations also are growing in membership and influence.

Most of the high ideals of both the junior high school and the middle school are reflected in the mission statements, publications, and conference programs of middle level professional organizations. Especially notable is the NMSA position paper, *This We Believe: Developmentally Responsive Middle Level Schools* (1995). If we keep visions like these constantly before us, we cannot go too far wrong in designing educational experiences for young people who are going through the critical transition years. In short, we might say:

> *Yes, you've come a long way, Baby, but you still have a long way to go!* ▶

References

Aikin, W. (1942). *The story of the eight year study.* New York: Harper.

Alexander, W.M., with Carr, D., & McAvoy, K. (1995). *Student-oriented curriculum: Asking the right questions.* Columbus, OH: National Middle School Association.

Alexander, W.M., & George, P. S. (1981, 1993). *The exemplary middle school.* New York: Holt, Rinehart, & Winston.

Arnold, J., & Stevenson, C. (1998). *Teachers' teaming handbook: A middle level planning guide.* Orlando, FL: Harcourt Brace.

Bair, M., & Woodward, R.G. (1964). *Team teaching in action.* Boston: Houghton Mifflin.

Burkhardt, R. (1985). How well do we say farewell? *In Transition, 2* (2), 9-12. (Journal of the New York State Middle School Association.)

Carnegie Council on Adolescent Development. (1989). *Turning points: Preparing American youth for the 21st century.* New York: Carnegie Corporation.

Compton, M.F., & Hawn, H. C. (1993). *Exploration: The total curriculum.* Columbus, OH: National Middle School Association.

Gruhn, W.T., & Douglass, H. R. (1947, 1956, 1971). *The modern junior high school.* New York: Ronald Press.

Lipka, R., Lounsbury, J.H., Toepfer, C.F. Jr., Vars, G.F., Alessi, S.J., & Kridel, C. (1998). *The Eight-Year Study revisited: Lessons from the past for the present.* Columbus, OH: National Middle School Association.

Lounsbury, J.H., & Clark, D.C., (1990). *Inside grade eight: From apathy to excitement.* Reston, VA: National Association of Secondary School Principals.

National Middle School Association. (1991). *NCATE-approved curriculum guidelines.* Columbus, OH: National Middle School Association.

National Middle School Association. (1995).*This we believe: Developmentally responsive middle level schools.* Columbus, OH: NMSA.

Nickerson, N.C. (1966). *Junior high schools are on the way out.* Danville, IL: Interstate.

Simmons, R.G., & Blyth, D.A. (1987). *Moving into adolescence: The impact of pubertal change and school context.* New York: A. de Gruyter.

Stevenson, C., & Carr, J.F. (Eds.) (1993). *Integrated studies in the middle grades: 'Dancing through walls.'* New York: Teachers College Press.

Tomlinson, C. A. (1995). *How to differentiate instruction in mixed-ability classes.* Arlington, VA: Association for Supervision and Curriculum Development.

Vars, G. F. (1984). The functions of middle level schools. In John H. Lounsbury (Ed.), *Perspectives: Middle school education, 1964 - 1984* (pp. 39-51). Columbus, OH: National Middle School Association.

Vars, G. F. (1989, 1997). Getting closer to middle level students: Options for teacher-adviser guidance programs. *Schools in the Middle, 6,* 1-6; *4,* 16-22.

Vars, G.F., & Rakow, S.R. (1993). Making connections: Integrative curriculum and the gifted student. *Roeper Review, 16* (1), 48-53.

Wheelock, A. (1992). *Crossing the tracks: How "untracking" can save America's schools.* New York: The New Press (W. W. Norton).

Wright, G.S., & Greer, E. S. (1963). The junior high school: A survey of grades 7-8-9 in junior and junior-senior high schools, 1959-60. *Office of Education Bulletin, 32.* Washington, DC: Government Printing Office.

MOVING FORWARD FROM THE PAST